THE
VEGETABLE
COOKBOOK

THE
VEGETABLE COOKBOOK

From the earth to the table

This edition published in 2011
LOVE FOOD is an imprint of Parragon Books Ltd

Parragon
Queen Street House
4 Queen Street
Bath BA1 1HE, UK

ISBN: 978-1-4454-5407-8

Introduction by Christine McFadden
Cover illustration by Georgina Luck, www.georginaluck.com

Printed in China

Notes for the Reader
This book uses metric, imperial, and US cup measurements. Follow the same units of measurement throughout; do not mix metric and imperial. All spoon measurements are level: teaspoons are assumed to be 5 ml, and tablespoons are assumed to be 15 ml. Unless otherwise stated, milk is assumed to be whole, eggs are large, individual vegetables are medium, and pepper is freshly ground black pepper.

The times given are an approximate guide only. Preparation times differ according to the techniques used by different people and the cooking times may also vary from those given. Optional ingredients, variations, or serving suggestions have not been included in the calculations.

Recipes using raw or very lightly cooked eggs should be avoided by infants, the elderly, pregnant women, convalescents, and anyone with a chronic illness. Pregnant and breast-feeding women are advised to avoid eating peanuts and peanut products. People with nut allergies should be aware that some of the prepared ingredients used in the recipes in this book may contain nuts. Always check the packaging before use.

Picture Acknowledgments
The publisher would like to thank Getty Images for permission to reproduce copyright material on the following pages: pages 2, 5 (all), 10, 12, 15, 16–17, 18, 19 (all), 21, 24–25, 34–35, 70–71, 108–109, 144–145, and 182–183.

Contents

Introduction

The last few years have seen a significant change in our attitude to vegetables. Thanks to modern cultivation techniques and a renewed interest in home-grown and heritage varieties, they have become the superstars of the kitchen.

This book shows you how to make the most of this cornucopia, explaining the nutritional benefits, purchasing options, what to look for in terms of freshness, and how best to store vegetables once you get them home. Also included are the benefits of seasonal eating accompanied by lists of what is in season and when. Vegetables are grouped according to botanical characteristics, and each of the five chapters begins with a directory describing them in detail.

The Benefits of Eating Vegetables

Vegetables come in a dazzling array of shapes, sizes, and flamboyant colors. They are also tasty, nutritious, and fun to cook, and if you grow your own, they are even more satisfying.

Now that a strong link between a diet high in vegetables and good health has been firmly established, there is almost universal agreement among government advisers that we should eat at least five portions of vegetables and fruit a day.

There is good reason to follow this advice. Vegetables are nutritional superfoods. Not only do they provide vitamins, minerals, and fiber, they are also packed with other therapeutic substances that scientists believe may help protect against chronic and life-threatening diseases, such as heart disease and cancer. Among the most important substances are antioxidants, a group that includes several minerals, vitamins C and E, and carotenoids—a pigment found mainly in vegetables with orange or red flesh but also in dark green leafy ones. Antioxidants protect the body by deactivating harmful free radicals that attack the nucleus of body cells, causing genetic changes that have been linked to cancer.

Leafy greens, such as kale, collard greens, and broccoli, are top of the league, along with red sweet peppers, carrots, and squash with orange flesh. They are all rich sources of carotenoids and vitamin C. Avocados are also rich in vitamin C, as well as vitamin E, and are said to improve the condition of the skin and hair.

Brussels sprouts, asparagus, and broccoli contain high levels of folic acid (sometimes called folate), one of the B vitamins needed for healthy red blood cells. The onion family is a major source of sulfur compounds, which may help suppress malignant tumors. Garlic is particularly rich in allicin, a substance thought to reduce health-threatening cholesterol levels.

Legumes, such as dried beans, peas, and lentils, are an excellent source of low-fat protein as well as complex carbohydrates, vitamins, minerals, and fiber.

Vegetables also provide vital minerals especially needed by women: calcium to maintain bone mass later in life, and iron to help prevent anemia. Spinach, collard greens, and watercress are particularly high in calcium and contain plenty of iron. Broccoli and green sweet peppers are also a good source of iron. Unfortunately, the iron in plants is thought to be less well absorbed than iron from animal sources, although vitamin C will help the body absorb it.

It's worth remembering that vitamin C and the B vitamins are water-soluble vitamins, which means they are partially destroyed by exposure to the air, light, and heat, and they also leach into the cooking water. For maximum nutritional benefit, store vegetables in a cool dark place, chop or peel them only when you are ready to use them, and eat them raw or lightly cooked. Steaming or stir-frying are the best options.

Types of Vegetables

Vegetables consist of a surprising number of different parts—shoots and stems, roots and tubers, buds, leaves, flowers, and seeds—all of which we eat, depending on the type. There are also fruit, such as tomatoes and avocados, that are not strictly vegetables but are usually thought of as such.

Mushrooms are important plant foods, too, although these are technically fungi rather than vegetables. It is this immense botanical variation that makes vegetables such an interesting part of our diet and an inspiration for the cook.

This book is split into the following five chapters with vegetables grouped according to their botanical characteristics.

Heat-loving vegetables

The first chapter focuses on well-known heat lovers, such as avocados, tomatoes, sweet peppers, chiles, and eggplants. Their "fruit" are eaten as vegetables, and these colorful products form the backbone of an huge number of tasty and nutritious dishes.

The chapter also includes summer and winter squash. Summer squash—zucchini, for example—have thin edible skin and are eaten whole, seeds and all, while still young and tender. Winter squash, such as butternut, are hollow with tough, inedible skin. Pumpkins are a popular type of winter squash that are invariably round with a flat bottom and orange skin.

Shoots, stems, roots, and tubers

The chapter includes vegetables grown for their shoots and stems—asparagus, fennel, and celery, for example—as well as the more common roots, such as beets, celeriac, carrots, and radishes. Tubers are a fleshy protuberance attached to an underground sideways-growing stem. They include potatoes, sweet potatoes, and Jerusalem artichokes.

Brassicas and leafy greens

Vital to health, the all-important brassica, or cabbage, family includes leafy greens, such as spinach, kale, and cabbage, as well as the Chinese bok choy. Brussels sprouts, which are technically leaf buds, are also part of the group, along with broccoli and cauliflower.

Other leafy greens are included, too, because they offer a wonderful variety of colors, textures, and flavors, ranging from slightly bitter chicory, endive, and radicchio, to peppery arugula and watercress, spinach, mild-tasting lettuce, colorful Swiss chard, and juicy Asian leaves, such as mizuna.

Mushrooms and the onion family

Growing from a network of underground spores, mushrooms come in an array of shapes and sizes, from the trumpet-shape orange chanterelle to the more somber flat-capped portobello mushroom. Cultivated varieties include closed-cup brown creminis, to clumps of thin-stemmed enoki, enormous portabellos, and Asian types, such as oyster and shiitake.

The onion family includes leeks, garlic, shallots, and numerous types of onion. Leeks and scallions are upward-growing stems covered with tightly packed, fleshy leaves and moist, pliable skin. Garlic, shallots. and regular onions are swollen bulbs, either single- or multicloved, covered with a papery dry skin. Garlic may be harvested early while the skin is still soft and silky, and the cloves are barely formed. At this stage, it is known as green garlic.

Beans, peas, lentils, and corn

The final chapter focuses on one of the most important vegetable groups: the seeds of pod-bearing vegetables from the legume family. These include peas and beans, both fresh and dried, as well as dried lentils and chickpeas. Fresh beans include green beans with edible fleshy pods, and those that need the pod removed before cooking—fava beans or fresh borlotti beans, for example. Bean sprouts are the power-packed shoots that emerge from the newly germinated embryo of mung beans.

Although not a legume, the chapter also includes corn. Corn is botanically classified as grass. The ears contain the kernels—the part we eat—which, in turn, contain the immature seeds of corn.

Buying Vegetables

Nowadays, supermarkets provide us with the widest choice of vegetables, usually with year-round availability. Much of the produce is packaged, prewashed, and already prepared—which is a great convenience for those leading action-packed lives.

For freshness and seasonality, however, it's hard to beat a good family farm or farm stand. The best grow their own vegetables and harvest them on a daily basis. The produce is not necessarily cheap, but it is generally of good quality. Farmers' markets are another option. The vegetables on sale are locally grown—within the county or a defined radius—and the grower is likely to be there to tell you about them.

An alternative for those with little time to visit a family farm is to join a Community Supported Agriculture (CSA) delivery service. A box of vegetables is delivered to your door on a regular basis. You do not necessarily know what will be in the box, but it will be a selection of whatever happens to be in season. You may need to find inspiring ways of cooking the same vegetable.

Organic vegetables

Organic vegetables are undeniably expensive—they are grown on a smaller scale than conventional produce, and production and transportation costs are, therefore, higher. Even so, many people prefer organic vegetables on the grounds that they have not been dowsed with artificial fertilizers and pesticides, nor have they been genetically modified. Increasing awareness of the connection between health and diet has also fueled demand.

Although there is a lack of conclusive evidence that organic vegetables are better for you, it's hard to deny that they are often tastier than conventionally grown produce. However, it is important to remember that this may well be due to the skill of the grower, or the particular vegetable variety, or simply because the vegetables have been grown locally, picked at the peak of ripeness, and sold immediately.

Growing your own

There are few greater pleasures than growing your own vegetables, harvesting them when you need to, and knowing that what you are eating is absolutely fresh. You also get to try varieties that aren't normally available in the stores.

Even if space is limited, a surprising number of vegetables can be grown in flowerpots and window boxes. Easiest and reliable croppers for the beginner are radishes, cherry tomatoes, peas, and green beans. Potatoes can be grown in a special deep bag, available from online suppliers and garden centers.

Salad greens are also rewarding crops—try arugula, upland cress, and some of the more colorful lettuce that are rarely seen in the stores. Herbs, such as chives, parsley, and thyme, are invaluable in the kitchen and easy to grow in flowerpots.

Checking for freshness

There is no knowing how long loose vegetables will remain fresh once you get them home. Prepared vegetables will usually be marked with an expiration date, but that is still no guarantee that they will last until then. Buying well within the date will help, as will knowing what to look for in terms of appearance.

Heat-loving vegetables

Avocado: Look for avocados that give slightly when pressed—a sign that they are ready to eat. Hard ones will ripen at room temperature within a few days.

Chile and sweet pepper: Look for firm chiles and sweet peppers with smooth skin. Avoid any with soft patches.

Cucumber: Look for firm, stiff cucumbers that do not feel spongy or flabby.

Eggplant: Look for firm-textured eggplants with glossy, smooth skin. Avoid any with brown patches.

Tomato: Look for firm tomatoes with smooth skin, preferably with the green calyx still attached.

Winter squash: Look for pumpkins and other winter squash that feel heavy for their size. Avoid any with soft spots or damaged skin.

Zucchini: Look for firm zucchini that feel heavy for their size. Avoid any with broken skin.

Shoots

Asparagus: Look for crisp spears with tightly closed tips. Avoid any with wrinkled stems or slimy tips.

Globe artichoke: Look for heads with stiff, tightly packed leaves.

Stems

Celery: Look for heads with crisp stalks. Avoid any with brown patches.

Fennel: Look for tightly packed bulbs, preferably with a few green fronds attached. Avoid any with brown patches.

Roots

Beet: Look for firm, round bulbs with leaves attached.

Carrot: Look for firm, brightly colored roots with fresh green leaves, if attached. Avoid any with sprouting yellow rootlets, cracks, small holes, or soft brown bruises.

Celeriac: Look for firm bulbs that feel heavy for their size. Avoid any with soft spots or rotting roots.

Radish: Look for small to medium bulbs, preferably with roots and leaves still attached. Avoid any that feel spongy when pinched.

Tubers

Jerusalem artichoke: Look for firm, undamaged tubers. Avoid any that are bruised or broken.

Potato: Look for firm, undamaged tubers. Avoid any that are sprouting or have green patches.

Sweet potato: Look for firm small to medium tubers.

Brassicas

Broccoli: Look for bright green bunches. Avoid any that are limp, yellowing, or cracked at the end of the stem.

Brussels sprouts: Look for firm, tightly packed buds. Avoid any with yellow leaves.

Cabbage: Look for heads that feel heavy for their size, with crisp leaves. Avoid any with yellowing outer leaves, and those that have been stripped.

Cauliflower: Look for tightly packed heads that are creamy in color with crisp outer leaves.

Kale and bok choy: Look for crisp, fresh leaves and firm stems. Avoid any that are limp or yellowing, or have bruised stems.

Spinach: Look for dewy fresh, dark green leaves. Avoid any that are bruised, yellowing, or slimy.

Leafy greens

Arugula, watercress, and other similar small greens: Look for fresh, bright green leaves. Avoid any that are yellowing or slimy.

Belgian endive: Look for firm, elongated heads. Avoid any with green tips or slimy brown marks.

Lettuce and chicory: Look for dewy fresh leaves and firm hearts.

Radicchio: Look for firm, tightly packed heads. Avoid any that have had the outer leaves removed.

Swiss chard: Look for crisp, fresh leaves and firm stems. Avoid any that are limp or yellowing, or have bruised stems.

Mushrooms

Cultivated and wild mushrooms: Look for clean, slightly damp caps that smell fresh. Avoid any that look dry or are slimy.

Onion family

Garlic, onions, and shallots: Look for plump, solid bulbs with tight skin.

Leeks: Look for small to medium firm, white shafts. Avoid any with heavily trimmed or yellowing tops.

Scallions: Look for firm, stiff stems with bright green tips. Avoid any that look dry or slimy.

Peas, beans, lentils, and corn

Bean sprouts: Look for fresh-looking shoots. Avoid any that are brown or slimy.

Fava beans: Look for small to medium pods. Avoid any with large bumps.

Green beans: Look for crisp pods with a satiny sheen. Avoid runner beans that are excessively fibrous or very long.

Peas: Look for crisp, green pods. Avoid any that are yellowing or fibrous.

Corn: Look for moist silks and husks, and soft, plump kernels. Husks should completely enclose the kernels.

Frozen vegetables

There is clear evidence that the longer fresh vegetables are stored, the more their valuable nutrients degrade. Since freezing usually takes place quickly after harvesting, when nutrients are at their peak, store-bought frozen vegetables are often a better bet than fresh ones that are out of season. Home-frozen vegetables are equally nutritious as long as they are in top condition at the time of freezing.

Most frozen vegetables can be stored for 9–12 months at 0°F/-18°C or below, although there will be some loss of quality as the months go by. Do not refreeze vegetables once thawed, because the texture will deteriorate.

Canned vegetables

Canned vegetables are an acceptable nutritional alternative to fresh or frozen vegetables, although there will be some loss of nutrients and texture because of the heat treatment involved in the canning process. Particularly useful are tomatoes, beans, chickpeas, and lentils.

Look for cans with labels that indicate no salt or sugar has been added. Rinse well before use and do not overcook when reheating. Always check the expiration date and throw out any cans that are rusty, dented, or swollen.

Dried vegetables

Some vegetables, such as tomatoes, can be purchased in dried form. These may need to be soaked in warm water for 20–30 minutes before use or may be packed in oil. Dried beans are also useful ingredients to have in your pantry. They are cheaper than canned beans, but they do need to be soaked overnight and then boiled from anywhere from 30 minutes to 2 hours, depending on the type and age of the bean.

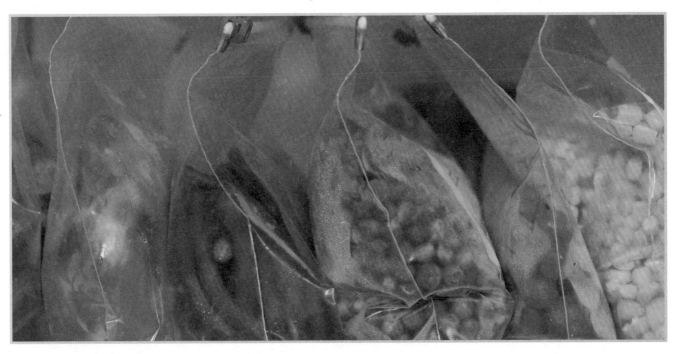

Seasonal Eating

Rightly or wrongly, in today's global market place we are no longer limited to vegetables that are in season. We can buy vegetables grown virtually anywhere in the world all year round, although often at the expense of flavor. Nowadays, however, many of us are opting to eat vegetables only when they are in season and, more often than not, only those grown locally, either within a county or defined radius. That way, we support local growers who transport their produce the shortest distance from plot to plate, and also help reduce the environmental damage potentially caused by shipping vegetables thousands of miles across the world.

A key advantage to seasonal eating is that you can enjoy vegetables when they are at their best and cheapest at the height of their natural harvest time. If there is a bumper crop, it is worth buying them in quantity and freezing the excess to be enjoyed at other times of the year.

Another advantage is that vegetables eaten in season are a real culinary treat as opposed to a slightly monotonous year-round feature on the menu. The first asparagus, early new potatoes, and young fava beans and peas are something to be eagerly relished after the relative bleakness of early spring. Tomatoes, zucchini, and sweet peppers are at their best in late summer, winter squash and pumpkins are a colorful reminder that fall is on its way, while parsnips and Brussels sprouts come into their own after the first frosts.

Eating seasonally helps put us in touch with natural rhythms of the culinary calendar. And by limiting your choice to what is in season, you are also more likely to experiment with unfamiliar varieties that you might otherwise not add to the menu.

What's in season

The following lists are an approximate guide to availability since weather conditions vary according to region. With the exception of cultivated mushrooms, the lists refer to outdoor crops instead of those grown in tunnels or under glass.

Spring

arugula
asparagus
cabbage
cauliflower
celeriac
collard greens
garlic (fresh, wild; *late spring*)
globe artichokes
kohlrabi *(mid- and late spring)*
leek *(early spring)*
lettuce
mushroom (wild morels, cultivated)
onion
parsnip *(early spring)*
pea *(mid- and late spring)*
potato
radicchio *(early spring)*
radish
scallion
shallot
snow pea *(mid- and late spring)*
spinach
watercress

Summer

arugula *(early summer)*
asparagus *(early summer)*
beet *(mid- and late summer)*
cabbage
carrot
celery
chiles
corn
cranberry bean *(fresh)*
cucumber
eggplant
fava bean *(early and midsummer)*
fennel
garlic *(fresh)*
green bean
kohlrabi
onion
parsley
pea *(early summer)*
potato
runner bean *(mid- and late summer)*
scallion
snow pea *(early summer)*
sweet pepper *(mid- and late summer)*
Swiss chard
tomato *(mid- and late summer)*
watercress
zucchini

Fall

Asian greens
Belgian endive *(late fall)*
beet
bok choy
Brussels sprouts
broccoli
cabbage
carrot
cauliflower
celeriac
celery *(early fall)*
chicory
chiles *(early fall)*
corn *(early fall)*
eggplant *(early fall)*
green bean *(early and mid fall)*
Jerusalem artichoke *(early and mid fall)*
kohlrabi *(early and mid fall)*
leek *(mid and late fall)*
lettuce
mushroom *(wild, cultivated)*
onion
parsnip
potato
pumpkin
radicchio *(late fall)*
radish
runner bean
rutabaga
shallot
spinach
sweet pepper *(early and mid fall)*
tomato *(early and mid fall)*
turnip
watercress
winter squash

Winter

Belgian endive
bok choy
Brussels sprouts
cabbage
carrot *(early and midwinter)*
cauliflower
celeriac
chicory
fava bean
Jerusalem artichoke
kale
leek
mushroom *(cultivated)*
onion
parsnip
potato
radicchio *(mid- and late winter)*
rutabaga
sweet potato
turnip
watercress

Storing Vegetables

From the moment of harvest, vegetables gradually start to deteriorate. Although they remain edible for a while, the flavor undergoes subtle changes, as does the texture, and they begin to lose valuable nutrients. Correct storage helps to slow down deterioration, so it is worth taking a few key principles onboard.

Many vegetables benefit from the humidity of the refrigerator crisper drawer, but others have different requirements. Tomatoes, for example, are best kept at room temperature because the chill of the refrigerator dulls the flavor. Similarly, the refrigerator is not a good place for onions, winter squash, and starchy root vegetables. These are best kept in a dark, dry, airy place, such as a cool pantry, or a ventilated drawer.

Packaging is also important. It's a good idea to keep your vegetables in a brown paper bag, or a ventilated plastic bag when storing them in the refrigerator. This provides the slightly humid but well-ventilated atmosphere that many vegetables need. However, a sealed plastic bag is better for watercress and fragile leafy greens that need an enclosed moist environment.

Freezing

Freezing is an excellent way to preserve vegetables, especially a bumper crop of homegrown ones. Most will keep for 9–12 months provided they are in peak condition at the time of freezing.

Prior to freezing, some vegetables should be blanched in boiling water to destroy enzymes that would otherwise speed up deterioration. Once blanched, cool quickly under running water, then drain and dry well before packing. Other vegetables, such as celery and sweet peppers, lose their crisp texture once thawed so are best used in stews and soups.

Vegetables that would benefit from blanching are indicated on this and the following pages, together with preparation tips and blanching times.

Heat-loving vegetables

Avocados: Store hard advocados at room temperature; they will ripen in 2–7 days. Store ripe ones in the refrigerator crisper drawer for 2–3 days.

Chiles and sweet peppers: Store in the refrigerator crisper drawer for up to 1 week. For the best flavor, bring to room temperature before using. Once cut, wrap tightly in plastic wrap and use within 24 hours. To freeze: Halve lengthwise and discard the stem and seeds. Broil the halves for 5–8 minutes, or slice thickly and blanch for 3 minutes.

Cucumbers: Store in the refrigerator crisper drawer for 3–4 days. Once cut, wrap tightly in plastic wrap and use within 24 hours.

Eggplant: Store in the refrigerator crisper drawer for 3–4 days.
To freeze: Cut into ¼-inch/5-mm slices and blanch for 3 minutes.

Pumpkin and other winter squash: Store in a dry, airy garage for 2–6 months, or at room temperature for 2–3 weeks.
To freeze: Cut into wedges and discard skin and seeds. Roast until tender, or cut into chunks, blanch for 3 minutes, then puree.

Tomato: Store ripe tomatoes at room temperature for 1–2 days. If not quite ripe, let stand to ripen, preferably on a sunny windowsill, for up to 1 week. Avoid storing in the refrigerator because the chill dulls the flavor.
To freeze: Chop and simmer in own juice for 5 minutes, then puree. Push through a strainer for a smoother puree.

Zucchini and other summer squash: Store in the refrigerator crisper drawer for 2–4 days.
To freeze: Trim and slice thickly. Blanch for 1 minute.

Shoots

Asparagus: Trim the ends and place upright in a glass of water loosely covered with a plastic bag. Store in the refrigerator for 1–2 days.
To freeze: Divide into thick and thin stems. Trim woody ends. Blanch thick stems for 4 minutes, thin stems for 2 minutes.

Globe artichoke: Wrap tightly in plastic wrap and store in the refrigerator crisper drawer for 2–3 days.

Stems

Celery: Store in the plastic sleeve in the refrigerator crisper drawer for up to 1 week. Once trimmed, wrap unused stems tightly in kitchen foil. Store for up to 3 days.

Fennel: Store in the refrigerator crisper drawer for up to 4 days. Once cut, wrap tightly in plastic wrap and use within 24 hours.

Roots

Beet: Remove leaves, leaving a small length of stem still attached. Store in the refrigerator crisper drawer for up to 1 week.

Carrot: Remove leaves, leaving a small length of stem still attached. Store in the refrigerator crisper drawer for up to 1 week. Store baby carrots for 1–2 days.
To freeze: Leave whole if small, slice thickly if large. Blanch for 3–5 minutes.

Celeriac: Store in a dry, airy garage for up to 2 weeks. Otherwise, wrap in plastic wrap and store in the refrigerator crisper drawer for up to 1 week.

Radish: Remove leaves, leaving a short length of stem still attached. Wrap in damp paper towels, unwashed. Store in a sealed plastic bag in the refrigerator crisper drawer for up to 1 week.

Tubers

Jerusalem artichoke: Store away from light in a dry, airy garage for 3–4 weeks. Alternatively, store in a cloth or paper bag in a well-ventilated drawer for up to 1 week.

Potato: Store away from light, in a dry, airy garage for 2–3 months. Alternatively, store in a cloth or paper bag in a well-ventilated drawer for up to 1 week.

Sweet potato: Store away from light in a dry, airy garage for 3–4 weeks. Alternatively, store in a cloth or paper pag in a well-ventilated drawer for up to 1 week.

Brassicas

Bok choy: Wrap in damp paper towels, unwashed. Store in a sealed plastic bag in the refrigerator crisper drawer for 1–2 days.

Broccoli and cauliflower: Store in the refrigerator crisper drawer for 2–3 days.
To freeze: Break into florets. Slice thick stems. Blanch for 3–5 minutes.

Brussels sprouts: Store in the refrigerator crisper drawer for 1–2 days.
To freeze: Trim ends. Blanch for 3–4 minutes.

Cabbage: Store uncut in the refrigerator crisper drawer for up to 1 week. Once cut, wrap unused portion tightly in plastic wrap and use within 1–2 days.

Kale: Trim tough stems. Wrap in damp paper towels, unwashed. Store in a sealed plastic bag in the refrigerator crisper drawer for 3–4 days.

Spinach: Wash and dry, then spread out on paper towels and roll up loosely. Store in a roomy sealed plastic bag in the refrigerator crisper drawer for 1–2 days.
To freeze: Trim tough stems. Blanch in small batches for 2 minutes. Squeeze out liquid before freezing.

Leafy greens
Arugula and other similar small leaves: Wash and dry, then spread out on paper towels and roll up loosely. Store in a roomy, sealed plastic bag in the refrigerator crisper drawer for 1–2 days.

Belgian endive: Store in the refrigerator crisper drawer for 2–3 days.

Lettuce, chicory, and radicchio: Store unwashed in the refrigerator crisper drawer for 3–4 days. Alternatively, wash and dry, then spread out on paper towels and roll up loosely. Store in a roomy, sealed plastic bag in the refrigerator crisper drawer for 1–2 days.

Swiss chard: Wrap in damp paper towels, unwashed. Store in a sealed plastic bag in the refrigerator crisper drawer for 1–2 days.

Watercress: Wrap bunched watercress in damp paper towels. Store in a sealed plastic bag in the refrigerator crisper drawer for 1–2 days.

Mushrooms
Cultivated and wild mushrooms: Store loosely wrapped in a brown paper bag in the refrigerator crisper drawer for 1–2 days.

Onion family
Garlic: Store in a clay garlic pot or in a ventilated drawer or vegetable rack for 7–10 days.

Leek: Store in the refrigerator crisper drawer for up to 1 week.

Onion and shallot: Store yellow onions and shallots in a cool, airy garage for several weeks. Alternatively, store in a ventilated drawer or vegetable rack for up to 10 days. Store white, red, and Bermuda onions for up to only 5–7 days because they rot more quickly.

Scallion: Store in the refrigerator crisper drawer for up to 1 week.

Peas, Beans, Lentils, and Corn
Bean sprouts: Store in a sealed plastic bag in the refrigerator crisper drawer for 1–2 days.

Corn: Keep husks intact and wrap in damp paper towels. Store in a sealed plastic bag in the refrigerator crisper drawer for up to 24 hours.

Fava beans: Store unshelled in the refrigerator crisper drawer for 2–3 days.
To freeze: Select small-to medium beans. Shell and blanch for 3 minutes.

Green beans: Store in the refrigerator crisper drawer for 3–4 days.
To freeze: Trim, removing any strings, if necessary. Cut green beans into pieces or leave whole. Slice runner beans. Blanch for 2–3 minutes.

Peas: Store unshelled in the refrigerator crisper drawer for 1–2 days.
To freeze: Select young tender peas. Shell and blanch for 1–2 minutes.

Preparing Vegetables

Although many supermarkets now sell prepared vegetables, it is much better to buy vegetables fresh and loose and to prepare them just before you need them. Wash or scrub everything, but do not let vegetables stay soaking in water or their water-soluble vitamins, such as vitamin C, will leach out. Similarly, do not cut or prepare vegetables too far in advance, as the water-soluble vitamins will diminish once the cut surface is exposed to the air.

How to peel and seed tomatoes

1. Cut the stem end out of each tomato using a sharp knife. Cut a cross in the skin of each tomato. Bring a large pan of water to a boil, then add the tomatoes. Let stand for 5–10 seconds, or until the tomato skins begin to loosen, then remove the tomatoes with a slotted spoon.
2. Place the tomatoes in a bowl of iced water to stop the cooking.
3. Drain the tomatoes and carefully remove the skins.
4. Cut the tomatoes into quarters, then remove and discard the seeds. Dice the flesh or cut into strips, as required.

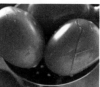

How to prepare sweet peppers

1. Wash the sweet peppers, then cut lengthwise in half.
2. Remove and discard the green stem.
3. Cut out the white membranes and any remaining seeds, then slice or chop as required.

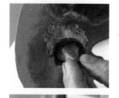

How to chop onions

1. Peel the onion and cut in half lengthwise.
2. Place the onion halves cut-side down on a cutting board. Cut the onion halves lengthwise, being careful not to cut through the root.
3. Turn the blade of the knife so it is parallel with the board and slice the onion, again leaving the root end intact.
4. Grip the onion firmly, then turn the knife again and cut widthwise across the original slices until you reach the root end.

How to prepare leeks

1. Remove and discard the root end from the leeks.
2. Trim the opposite end of the leeks, discarding the dark green leaves.
3. Peel off the outer layer of the leeks.
4. Wash the leeks under cold running water to remove any dirt, then slice or chop as required.

How to prepare a pumpkin or squash

1. Cut the pumpkin or squash widthwise in half, then spoon the seeds into a bowl and set aside.
2. Cut the flesh into wedges and peel off the skin.
3. Remove and discard the stringy insides using a sharp knife.
4. Cut the pumpkin or squash wedges into ½-inch/1-cm chunks.
5. If desired, the seeds can be roasted at 325°F/160°C for 30 minutes. Sprinkle with salt to taste before serving.

How to prepare celery

1. Remove and discard the root end of the celery and trim the leaf end.
2. Wash the celery stalks well under cold running water.
3. Remove the strings using a sharp knife or vegetable peeler, then slice or chop the celery as required.

How to prepare fennel

1. Remove and discard the root end of the fennel.
2. Peel off the outer layers.
3. Trim off the stalks and leaves. The leaves can be used as a garnish and the stalks may be used in sauces and stocks.
4. Slice the bulb in half through the root, then slice or chop the fennel as required.

How to prepare mushrooms

1. Trim the mushroom stems, removing any dirt.
2. Wipe the mushrooms with a sheet of damp paper towel, then slice or chop as required.

How to prepare spinach

1. Wash the spinach under cold running water. Remove and discard any yellow leaves.
2. Remove and discard the stems.

Essential Cooking Techniques

While most vegetables can be eaten raw, there are numerous cooking techniques that will add interest and variety to your meals. You can maximize the flavor, color, and texture of the vegetables, while preserving as much of the essential vitamins and nutrients as possible.

Boiling

The traditional method of cooking vegetables is to use plenty of salted water and a large uncovered saucepan. This method is most suitable for corn, potatoes, and other root vegetables. Although steaming is preferable when cooking green vegetables because they retain more nutrients, if you choose to boil them, boil them uncovered; if you put the lid on, they will lose their attractive bright green color. Choose a saucepan in a size appropriate for the quantity of vegetables so that the water can circulate, but use the minimum amount of water, cook for the briefest period, and drain the vegetables immediately because boiling destroys the water-soluble vitamin C and B vitamins. Other water-soluble nutrients leach into the cooking water, so get into the habit of keeping the cooking water and using it as a base for soup or sauces.

Poaching

A less vigorous way to cook more delicate vegetables is to put them in boiling liquid (water, stock, wine, or milk), then to simmer them gently over low heat to retain their flavor, texture, and shape.

Frying

Deep-frying is less popular these days, with concerns over the amount of fat in our diet. In fact, if the cooking temperature is correct, deep-fried foods are quickly sealed and absorb less oil than when they are shallow-fried. Coating vegetables in batter or in egg and breadcrumbs forms a crispy seal, which also reduces oil absorption. Deep-frying is a long-established cooking method for potatoes (fries) and also works well for eggplants and zucchini. Dry-frying in a skillet or ridged grill pan or on a flat griddle plate is a healthier option that can be used for some vegetables.

Steaming

Less water comes into contact with vegetables when they are steamed instead of boiled, so they are crispy and retain more essential nutrients. Also, some vegetables—snow peas, leeks, and zucchini—become limp and unappetizing if boiled. Steamed new potatoes are particularly delicious; try putting some fresh mint leaves under the potatoes to flavor them while they are steaming.

Braising

This cooking method requires only a very little water, and the saucepan is covered. The heat is much reduced and the cooking time greatly increased. You can start by browning the ingredients in a little oil or butter, then add water or other liquid before covering the saucepan. The small amount of liquid that remains at the end of the cooking will be sweet and flavored—serve the vegetables with this juice and you gain all the nutrients. Onions, turnips, leeks, chicory, celery, and fennel lend themselves to braising. Red cabbage is one of the brassicas that positively benefits from this long, slow method of cooking.

Stir-frying

This method of frying in a little oil over high heat has become widely popular. Stir-fried vegetables retain far more of their nutritional value, flavor, texture, and

color. They are thinly sliced and rapidly moved around in a hot wok to aid fast and even cooking. Most of us are familiar with stir-fried baby corn, snow peas, bell peppers, bean sprouts, and bamboo shoots, but the method is an equally good way to cook thinly sliced cauliflower, Brussels sprouts, cabbage, and carrots.

Roasting

Traditionally, roasting vegetables meant cooking them in the fat dripping from a meat roast. The much healthier option is to roast vegetables that have been lightly drizzled with olive oil in a roasting pan, to which you can add garlic and herbs for additional flavor. Squash, parsnips, potatoes, bell peppers, onions, tomatoes, asparagus, and even beets are all delicious cooked in this way; their flavor is concentrated and the natural sweetness of the vegetables is accentuated.

Sautéing and sweating

These methods use less oil than traditional shallow-frying and are longer, slower processes than stir-frying. Sautéing is done in an uncovered skillet; sweating in either a heavy-bottom lidded casserole or skillet—water evaporating from the ingredients is trapped and falls back into the pan. Onions are often sweated to soften them without coloring.

Baking

Potatoes, onions, and garlic can be baked "dry" in their skins, while softer vegetables (such as bell peppers and tomatoes) can be stuffed with rice or other filling or wrapped in foil and baked.

Broiling and grilling

Broiling and grilling are both dry-heat cooking methods that are similar to each other, with the former cooking from the top and the latter from the bottom. The intense heat from a broiler or barbecue is unsuitable for either delicate or dense vegetables, which become charred instead of cooked, but excellent for softer ones, such as onions, corn, bell peppers, eggplants, and tomatoes. All vegetables need to be brushed with oil before being placed on the broiler rack or grill rack.

Cooking times

For maximum nutritional benefit, it makes sense to cook your vegetables for the least amount of time possible. Cut them the same size so that they look attractive and cook evenly. While potatoes have to be cooked all the way through, other root vegetables, such as carrots, are best served with a little "bite" to them. Boil for less time or steam your vegetables and enjoy the extra crunch. Some vegetables—those with a high-water content, such as spinach, celery, or bean sprouts—need to be only blanched in boiling water for 30 seconds. For frying and stir-frying, make sure that the oil is properly hot before adding the vegetables. When time is short, try microwaving your vegetables. This method requires less liquid or fat, and results in shorter cooking times than conventional cooking.

Chapter 1
Heat-Loving Vegetables

Directory of Heat-Loving Vegetables

The vegetables in this group all prefer hot climates. They are all also technically fruits but are normally treated as vegetables. These vegetables are incredibly versatile—they are suitable for the majority of cooking methods and some of them can also be eaten raw.

Avocado

With their rich, nutty flavor and buttery texture, avocados are ideal for eating raw. They are eaten straight from the skin, added to salads, or pureed with zesty seasonings to make guacamole or other dips. Avocados can also be baked or used in a rich, creamy soup.

Chile

Chiles have a crucial role in many cuisines, particularly Mexican, Indian, and Thai. There are hundreds of different types, ranging in potency from mildly piquant to blisteringly hot. Chiles can be fried, roasted, or broiled, added to soups and stews, or used to perk up starchy vegetables, beans, and grain dishes.

Cucumber

The cooling nature of cucumbers comes into its own in Indian and Middle Eastern cuisines. Here they are traditionally combined with yogurt and mint to make soothing sauces and dips to offset the heat of spicy dishes. Smooth-skinned types have tender skin and do not need peeling. Spiny ridge cucumbers have tough bitter skin that must be removed. Cucumbers are best eaten raw. They add color and texture to salads and they also make excellent pickles.

Eggplant

Known in the Middle East as "poor man's caviar," eggplants provide substance and flavor to spicy stews and tomato-base bakes. They can be roasted, broiled, or pureed into garlicky dips.

Pumpkin and other winter squash

Large pumpkins are probably best kept for making lanterns at Halloween, but small pumpkins have a sweeter, less fibrous flesh that is good for baking pies, and can be roasted, baked, and used in soups and stews. Butternut squash, however, is one of the most readily available winter types. A large, distinctively pear-shaped vegetable with a golden skin and orange flesh, it is equally delicious mashed, baked, or roasted, or used in soups and stews.

Sweet pepper

Bell peppers are by far the most common type of sweet pepper, and they come in a spectrum of colors, starting off grassy green, then maturing to yellow, orange, and vibrant red. Some varieties are rich purple or even chocolate brown. They all add substance and color to many kinds of soups, salads, stews, and stir-fries. They can also be stuffed with meat or rice, broiled as an appetizer, or pureed for dips and sauces.

Tomato

There are now so many varieties from which to choose, from the sweet bite-size cherry to the large, beefy slicing tomato. With its thick, juicy flesh, the egg-shape plum tomato is perfect for rich sauces, while sun-dried tomatoes add intense flavor to dips, sauces, soups, and stews.

Zucchini and other summer squash

One of the best-known types of summer squash is the zucchini. They are at their best when small and young; the flavor diminishes and the seeds toughen as they grow older and larger. Extremely versatile, zucchini can be steamed, stir-fried, pureed, grilled, and roasted, as well as used in soups and casseroles. Their deep yellow flowers are perfect for stuffing. Other popular types of summer squash include yellow squash and scallop squash.

Tomato Bruschetta

Serves 4

ingredients

- 8 slices rustic bread
- 4 garlic cloves, halved
- 8 plum tomatoes, peeled and diced
- extra virgin olive oil, for drizzling
- salt and pepper
- fresh basil leaves, to garnish

1 Preheat the broiler. Lightly toast the bread on both sides. Rub each piece of toast with half of a garlic clove and then return to the broiler for a few seconds.

2 Divide the diced tomatoes among the toasts. Season to taste with salt and pepper and drizzle with oil. Serve immediately, garnished with basil leaves.

Polenta with Tomatoes &
Garlic Sauce

Serves 4

ingredients
- 3 cups vegetable stock or water
- ¾ cup instant polenta or coarse cornmeal
- 2 tbsp butter
- 3 tbsp snipped fresh chives
- 2 tbsp chopped fresh flat-leaf parsley
- olive oil, for brushing
- 4 plum tomatoes, sliced
- salt and pepper

garlic sauce
- 2 thick slices French bread, crusts removed
- 3 garlic cloves, chopped
- ½ tsp salt
- 1 cup walnut pieces
- 3 tbsp lemon juice
- scant ½ cup olive oil

1 Bring the stock to a boil in a large saucepan. Add the polenta and cook over medium heat, stirring continuously, for 5 minutes, until it starts to come away from the sides of the pan.

2 Remove the pan from the heat and beat in the butter, chives, and parsley and season to taste with pepper. Pour the polenta into an oiled dish and spread out evenly. Let cool and set.

3 To make the garlic sauce, tear the bread into pieces and place in a bowl. Cover with cold water and let soak for 10 minutes. Pound the garlic cloves with the salt to make a paste. Work in the walnuts. Squeeze out the bread, work it into the paste, then add the lemon juice. Stir in the oil until the sauce is thick and creamy. Transfer to a bowl, cover with plastic wrap, and set aside.

4 Brush a ridged grill pan with oil and heat. Cut the set polenta into wedges or rounds. Season the tomatoes with salt and pepper. When the grill pan is hot, add the polenta and tomatoes and cook for 4–5 minutes.

5 Divide the polenta and tomatoes among warm plates and spoon the garlic sauce over the top. Serve immediately.

Avocado &
Almond Soup

Serves 4

ingredients
- 2½ cups water
- 1 onion, finely chopped
- 1 celery stalk, finely chopped
- 1 carrot, grated
- 4 garlic cloves, chopped or crushed
- 1 bay leaf
- ½ tsp salt, or to taste
- 1 cup ground almonds
- 2 ripe avocados (about 1 lb/450 g)
- 3–4 tbsp lemon juice
- extra virgin olive oil, for drizzling
- snipped fresh chives, to garnish

1 Combine the water, onion, celery, carrot, garlic, bay leaf, and salt in a pan. Bring to a boil, reduce the heat, cover, and simmer for about 30 minutes, or until the vegetables are tender.

2 Strain the mixture, reserving the liquid and the vegetables separately. Remove and discard the bay leaf.

3 Put the vegetables into a blender or food processor. Add the almonds and a small amount of the liquid and process to a very smooth puree, scraping down the sides as necessary. Add as much of the remaining liquid as the capacity of the blender or processor permits and process to combine. Scrape into a bowl, stir in any remaining liquid, cover, and chill in the refrigerator until cold.

4 Cut the avocados in half, discard the pits, and scoop the flesh into the blender or food processor. Add the cold soup base and process to a smooth puree, scraping down the sides as necessary. For a thinner consistency, add a few spoonfuls of cold water.

5 Add the lemon juice and season to taste with salt. Ladle into chilled bowls and drizzle with extra virgin olive oil. Serve immediately, garnished with chives.

Pasta Salad with
Charbroiled Bell Peppers

Serves 4

ingredients
- 1 red bell pepper
- 1 orange bell pepper
- 10 oz/280 g dried conchiglie
- 5 tbsp extra virgin olive oil
- 2 tbsp lemon juice
- 2 tbsp pesto
- 1 garlic clove, finely chopped
- 3 tbsp shredded fresh basil leaves
- salt and pepper

1 Preheat the broiler. Put the whole bell peppers on a baking sheet and place under the hot broiler, turning frequently, for 15 minutes, or until charred all over. Remove with tongs and place in a bowl. Cover with crumpled paper towels and reserve.

2 Meanwhile, bring a large saucepan of lightly salted water to a boil. Add the pasta, return to a boil, and cook for 8–10 minutes, or according to the package directions, until the pasta is tender but still firm to the bite.

3 Combine the oil, lemon juice, pesto, and garlic in a large bowl, whisking well to mix. Drain the pasta, add it to the oil mixture while still hot, and toss well. Reserve until required.

4 When the bell peppers are cool enough to handle, peel off the skins, then cut open and remove the seeds. Chop the flesh coarsely and add to the pasta with the basil. Season to taste with salt and pepper and toss well. Serve.

Summer Vegetable &
Herb Tart

Serves 4–6

ingredients
- 2 red bell peppers
- 4 tbsp olive oil
- 12 oz/350 g prepared puff pastry, thawed if frozen
- all-purpose flour, for dusting
- 2 ripe but firm tomatoes, thinly sliced
- 9 oz/250 g ricotta cheese
- 1 cup grated Parmesan cheese
- 1 tsp fresh thyme leaves
- 1 tbsp snipped fresh chives
- salt and pepper

1 Preheat the oven to 400°F/200°C.

2 Remove the stems and seeds from the red bell peppers and cut the flesh into thin strips. Transfer to a baking sheet and drizzle with half of the oil. Season to taste with salt and pepper and roast in the preheated oven for 20 minutes, or until soft. Remove from the oven and let cool while you prepare the tart shell.

3 Roll the pastry out on a floured work surface and use to line a 9-inch/23-cm tart pan. Prick the bottom with a fork to prevent the pastry from puffing up.

4 Scatter the roasted bell peppers evenly over the bottom of the tart shell, then arrange the tomato slices on top and season to taste with salt and pepper.

5 Beat the ricotta cheese in a bowl until smooth, then spoon over the vegetables. Sprinkle with the Parmesan cheese, thyme, and chives, then drizzle with the remaining oil. Bake in the preheated oven for 20 minutes, or until the pastry and cheese topping are golden. Serve immediately or let cool.

Ratatouille

Serves 4

ingredients
- 2 eggplants
- 4 zucchini
- 2 yellow bell peppers
- 2 red bell peppers
- 2 onions
- 2 garlic cloves
- ⅔ cup olive oil
- 1 bouquet garni
- 3 large tomatoes, peeled, seeded, and coarsely chopped
- salt and pepper

1 Coarsely chop the eggplants and zucchini, and seed and chop the bell peppers. Slice the onions and finely chop the garlic.

2 Heat the oil in a large saucepan. Add the onions and cook over low heat, stirring occasionally, for 5 minutes, or until softened. Add the garlic and cook, stirring frequently, for an additional 2 minutes.

3 Add the eggplants, zucchini, and bell peppers. Increase the heat to medium and cook, stirring occasionally, until the bell peppers begin to color. Add the bouquet garni, reduce the heat, cover, and simmer gently for 40 minutes.

4 Stir in the tomatoes and season to taste with salt and pepper. Re-cover the saucepan and simmer gently for an additional 10 minutes. Remove and discard the bouquet garni. Serve warm or cold.

Chili Tofu Tortillas

Serves 4

ingredients

- ½ tsp chili powder
- 1 tsp paprika
- 2 tbsp all-purpose flour
- 1 cup ½-inch/1-cm firm tofu
  ·pieces
- 2 tbsp vegetable oil
- 1 onion, finely chopped
- 1 garlic clove, crushed
- 1 large red bell pepper, seeded
  and finely chopped
- 1 large ripe avocado
- 1 tbsp lime juice
- 4 tomatoes, peeled, seeded. and
  chopped
- 1 cup grated cheddar cheese
- 8 soft flour tortillas
- ⅔ cup sour cream
- salt and pepper
- pickled green jalapeño chiles,
  to serve

sauce

- 3½ cups sugocasa
  (see page 52)
- 3 tbsp chopped fresh parsley
- 3 tbsp chopped fresh cilantro

1 Preheat the oven to 375°F/190°C. Mix the chlli powder, paprika, flour, and salt and pepper to taste on a plate and use to coat the tofu pieces.

2 Heat the oil in a skillet and gently fry the tofu for 3–4 minutes, until golden. Remove with a slotted spoon, drain on paper towels, and set aside.

3 Add the onion, garlic, and bell pepper to the oil and fry for 2–3 minutes, until just soft. Drain and set aside.

4 Halve the avocado, peel, and remove the pit. Slice lengthwise, put in a bowl with the lime juice, and toss to coat.

5 Add the tofu and the onion mixture and gently stir in the tomatoes and half of the cheese. Spoon a little of the filling down the center of each tortilla, top with a little sour cream, and roll up.

6 Arrange the tortillas in a shallow ovenproof dish in a single layer.

7 To make the sauce, mix all the ingredients together. Spoon the sauce over the tortillas, sprinkle with the remaining cheese, and bake in the preheated oven for 25 minutes, until the cheese is golden brown and bubbling.

8 Serve the tortillas immediately with the pickled jalapeño chiles.

Pasta all'Arrabbiata

Serves 4

ingredients
- ⅔ cup dry white wine
- 1 tbsp sun-dried tomato paste
- 2 fresh red chiles
- 2 garlic cloves, finely chopped
- 12 oz/350 g dried tortiglioni
- ¼ chopped fresh flat-leaf parsley
- salt and pepper
- pecorino cheese shavings,
  to garnish

sugocasa
- 5 tbsp extra virgin olive oil
- 2½ cups chopped plum tomatoes
- salt and pepper

1 For the sugocasa, heat the oil in a skillet over high heat until almost smoking. Add the tomatoes and cook, stirring frequently, for 2–3 minutes. Reduce the heat to low and cook gently for 20 minutes, or until soft. Season to taste with salt and pepper. Using a wooden spoon, press through a nonmetallic strainer into a saucepan.

2 Add the wine, sun-dried tomato paste, whole chiles, and garlic to the sugocasa and bring to a boil. Reduce the heat and simmer gently.

3 Meanwhile, bring a large saucepan of lightly salted water to a boil. Add the pasta, return to a boil, and cook for 8–10 minutes, or according to the package directions, until the pasta is tender but still firm to the bite.

4 Remove the chiles and taste the sauce. If you prefer a hotter flavor, chop up some or all of the chiles and return to the saucepan. Check and adjust the seasoning, adding salt and pepper if needed, then stir in half of the parsley.

5 Drain the pasta and transfer to a warm serving bowl. Add the sauce and toss to coat. Sprinkle with the remaining parsley, garnish with the pecorino cheese shavings, and serve immediately.

Stuffed Eggplants

Serves 4

ingredients

- 8 oz/225 g dried penne or other short pasta shapes
- 4 tbsp olive oil, plus extra for brushing
- 2 eggplants
- 1 large onion, chopped
- 2 garlic cloves, crushed
- 14 oz/400 g canned chopped tomatoes
- 2 tsp dried oregano
- 2 oz/55 g mozzarella cheese, thinly sliced
- ¼ cup grated Parmesan cheese
- scant ⅓ cup dried breadcrumbs
- salt and pepper

1 Preheat the oven to 400°F/200°C. Bring a large saucepan of lightly salted water to a boil. Add the pasta and 1 tablespoon of the oil, return to a boil, and cook for 8–10 minutes, or according to the package directions, until the pasta is tender but still firm to the bite. Drain, return to the pan, cover, and keep warm.

2 Cut the eggplants in half lengthwise and score around the inside with a sharp knife, being careful not to pierce the skins. Scoop out the flesh with a spoon. Brush the insides with oil. Chop the flesh and set aside.

3 Heat the remaining oil in a skillet. Fry the onion over low heat for 5 minutes, until soft. Add the garlic and fry for about 1 minute. Add the chopped eggplant and fry, stirring frequently, for 5 minutes. Add the tomatoes and oregano and season to taste with salt and pepper. Bring to a boil and simmer for 10 minutes, until thickened. Remove the skillet from the heat and stir in the pasta.

4 Brush a baking sheet with oil and arrange the eggplant shells in a single layer. Divide half of the tomato-and-pasta mixture among them. Scatter on the mozzarella cheese, then pile the remaining tomato-and-pasta mixture on top. Mix together the Parmesan cheese and breadcrumbs and sprinkle over the top, patting lightly into the mixture.

5 Bake in the preheated oven for about 25 minutes, or until the topping is golden brown. Serve immediately.

Eggplant Curry

Serves 2

ingredients

- 2 tbsp peanut or vegetable oil, plus extra for deep-frying
- 2 eggplants, cut into ¾-inch/2-cm cubes
- 1 bunch scalliions, coarsely chopped
- 2 garlic cloves, chopped
- 2 red bell peppers, seeded and cut into ¾-inch/2-cm squares
- 3 zucchini, thickly sliced
- 14 fl oz/400 ml canned coconut milk
- 2 tbsp Thai red curry paste
- large handful fresh cilantro, chopped, plus extra sprigs to garnish
- cooked rice, to serve

1 Heat enough oil for deep-frying in a wok or a deep saucepan to 350–375°F/180–190°C, or until a cube of bread browns in 30 seconds. Add the eggplant cubes, in batches, and cook for 45 seconds–1 minute, until crisp and brown all over. Remove with a slotted spoon and drain on paper towels.

2 Heat the 2 tablespoons of oil in a separate wok or large skillet, add the scallions and garlic, and stir-fry over medium–high heat for 1 minute. Add the bell peppers and zucchini and stir-fry for 2–3 minutes.

3 Add the coconut milk and curry paste and bring gently to a boil, stirring occasionally. Add the eggplants and chopped cilantro, reduce the heat, and simmer for 2–3 minutes.

4 Serve immediately with rice, garnished with cilantro sprigs.

Curried Zucchini Soup

Serves 4

ingredients

- ½ tbsp butter
- 1 large onion, finely chopped
- 6 zucchini (about 2 lb/900 g), sliced
- 2 cups vegetable stock
- 1 tsp curry powder
- ½ cup sour cream, plus extra to serve
- salt and pepper

1 Melt the butter in a large saucepan over medium heat. Add the onion and cook for about 3 minutes, until it begins to soften.

2 Add the zucchini, stock, and curry powder, and season to taste with salt. Bring the soup to a boil, reduce the heat, cover, and cook gently for 25 minutes, until the vegetables are tender.

3 Let the soup cool slightly, then transfer to a food processor or blender, working in batches, if necessary. Process the soup until just smooth but still with green flecks. (If using a food processor, strain off the cooking liquid and reserve. Process the soup solids with enough cooking liquid to moisten them, then combine with the remaining liquid.)

4 Return the soup to the rinsed-out saucepan and stir in the sour cream. Reheat gently over low heat just until hot. (Do not boil.)

5 Taste and adjust the seasoning, adding salt and pepper, if needed. Ladle into warm bowls, top with a spoonful of sour cream, and serve.

Zucchini & Basil Risotto

Serves 4

ingredients

- 6 cups vegetable stock
- 4 tbsp basil-flavored extra virgin olive oil, plus extra for drizzling
- 4 zucchini, diced
- 1 yellow bell pepper, seeded and diced
- 2 garlic cloves, finely chopped
- 1 large onion, finely chopped
- 2 cups risotto rice
- 4 tbsp dry white vermouth
- 2 tbsp unsalted butter
- large handful fresh basil leaves, torn, plus extra to garnish
- heaping ¾ cup grated Parmesan cheese
- salt and pepper

1 Bring the stock to a boil in a medium saucepan, then reduce the heat and keep simmering gently over low heat while you cook the risotto.

2 Heat half of the oil in a large skillet over high heat. When very hot, but not smoking, add the zucchini and yellow bell pepper and stir-fry for 3 minutes, until lightly golden. Stir in the garlic and cook for an additional 30 seconds. Transfer to a plate and set aside.

3 Heat the remaining oil in a deep saucepan over medium heat. Add the onion and cook, stirring occasionally, for about 2 minutes, until soft. Add the rice and cook, stirring frequently, for about 2 minutes, until the rice is translucent and well coated with the oil.

4 Pour in the vermouth; it will simmer and steam rapidly and evaporate almost immediately.

5 Gradually add the hot stock, a ladleful at a time, stirring continuously. Add more stock as the rice absorbs each addition. Increase the heat so the liquid simmers. Cook for 20–25 minutes, or until all the liquid has been absorbed and the rice is creamy but still firm to the bite.

6 Stir in the zucchini mixture with any juices, the butter, basil, and Parmesan cheese. Season to taste with salt and pepper. Drizzle with a little oil and garnish with basil. Serve immediately.

Summer Squash
Ribbon Salad

Serves 4–6

ingredients
- 2 green zucchini
- 2 yellow squash
- 1 large carrot
- 1 cup thinly sliced radishes
- 4–6 scallions, chopped
- 2–3 tbsp shredded fresh basil leaves

dressing
- 4 tbsp extra virgin olive oil
- 1 tbsp lemon juice (or white wine vinegar)
- ½–1 tsp Dijon mustard
- 1 small garlic clove, crushed (optional)
- salt and pepper

1 To make the dressing, place the oil, lemon juice, mustard, garlic, if using, and salt and pepper to taste in a small bowl and whisk together until thoroughly mixed. Set aside.

2 Using a vegetable peeler, cut the zucchini and yellow squash into long, thin ribbons, avoiding the seeds in the center (discard the seedy cores). Place in a salad bowl.

3 Repeat with the carrot to make long, thin ribbons, then add these to the bowl together with the radishes, scallions, and basil. Toss gently to mix.

4 Give the dressing a quick whisk, then drizzle it over the salad and toss gently to coat. Serve immediately.

Roasted Butternut Squash

Serves 4

ingredients

- 1 butternut squash
- 1 onion, chopped
- 2–3 garlic cloves, crushed
- 4 small tomatoes, chopped
- 1⅓ cups chopped cremini mushrooms
- 3 oz/85 g canned lima beans, drained, rinsed, and coarsely chopped
- 1 cup grated zucchini
- 1 tbsp chopped fresh oregano, plus extra to garnish
- 2 tbsp tomato paste
- 1¼ cups water
- 4 scallions, chopped
- 1 tsp hot pepper sauce
- pepper

1 Preheat the oven to 375°F/190°C. Prick the squash all over with a skewer, then roast in the preheated oven for 40 minutes, or until tender. Remove from the oven and let stand until cool enough to handle.

2 Cut the squash in half lengthwise and scoop out and discard the seeds, then scoop out some of the flesh, leaving a ½-inch/1-cm border all around. Chop the scooped-out flesh and put in a bowl. Place the squash halves side by side in a large roasting pan.

3 Add the onion, garlic, tomatoes, and mushrooms to the squash flesh in the bowl. Add the lima beans, zucchini, oregano, and pepper to taste and mix well. Spoon the filling into the two squash halves, packing it down as firmly as possible.

4 Mix the tomato paste with the water, scallions, and hot pepper sauce in a small bowl and pour around the squash.

5 Cover loosely with a large sheet of foil and bake for 30 minutes, or until piping hot. Serve in warm bowls, garnished with oregano.

Penne with Pumpkin Sauce

Serves 4

ingredients
- 4 tbsp unsalted butter
- ¾ cup finely chopped white onions or shallots
- 1 lb 12 oz/800 g pumpkin
- freshly grated nutmeg
- 12 oz/350 g dried penne
- scant 1 cup light cream
- ¼ cup grated Parmesan cheese
- 2 tbsp chopped fresh flat-leaf parsley
- salt and pepper

1 Melt the butter in a heavy-bottom saucepan over low heat. Add the onions, sprinkle with a little salt, cover, and cook, stirring frequently, for 25–30 minutes.

2 Scoop out and discard the pumpkin seeds. Peel and finely chop the flesh. Turn the pumpkin into the saucepan and season to taste with nutmeg. Cover and cook over low heat, stirring occasionally, for 45 minutes.

3 Meanwhile, bring a large saucepan of lightly salted water to a boil. Add the pasta, return to a boil, and cook for 8–10 minutes, or according to the package directions, until the pasta is tender but still firm to the bite. Drain thoroughly, reserving about ⅔ cup of the cooking liquid.

4 Stir the cream, cheese, and parsley into the pumpkin sauce and season to taste with salt and pepper. If the mixture seems a little too thick, add some or all of the reserved cooking liquid and stir. Turn in the pasta and toss well. Serve immediately.

Pumpkin Chestnut Risotto

Serves 4

ingredients
- 4 cups vegetable stock
- 1 tbsp olive oil
- 3 tbsp butter
- 1 small onion, finely chopped
- 2 cups diced pumpkin
- 8 oz/225 g chestnuts, cooked and shelled
- 1½ cups risotto rice
- ⅔ cup dry white wine
- 1 tsp crumbled saffron threads (optional)
- heaping ¾ cup grated Parmesan cheese, plus extra to serve
- salt and pepper

1 Bring the stock to a boil, then reduce the heat and keep simmering gently over low heat while you cook the risotto.

2 Heat the oil with 2 tablespoons of the butter in a deep saucepan over medium heat until the butter has melted. Stir in the onion and pumpkin and cook, stirring occasionally, for 5 minutes, or until the onion is soft and starting to turn golden and the pumpkin begins to color. Coarsely chop the chestnuts and add to the mixture. Stir thoroughly to coat.

3 Reduce the heat, add the rice, and mix to coat in oil and butter. Cook, stirring continuously, for 2–3 minutes, or until the grains are translucent. Add the wine and cook, stirring continuously, for 1 minute, until it has reduced. If using the saffron threads, dissolve them in ¼ cup of the hot stock and add the liquid to the rice after the wine has been absorbed. Cook, stirring continuously, until the liquid has been absorbed.

4 Gradually add the hot stock, a ladleful at a time, stirring continuously. Add more liquid as the rice absorbs each addition. Increase the heat to medium so that the liquid simmers. Cook for 20 minutes, or until all the liquid has been absorbed and the rice is creamy but still firm to the bite.

5 Remove the risotto from the heat and add the remaining butter. Mix well, then stir in the Parmesan until it melts. Adjust the seasoning, adding salt and pepper, if needed. Spoon the risotto onto warm plates and serve immediately, sprinkled with Parmesan.

Chapter 2
Shoots, Stems, Roots & Tubers

Directory of Shoots, Stems, Roots & Tubers

The vegetables in this group grow either below the soil or shoot up above it. Between them, they form the base for all kinds of dishes, from summery appetizers and salads to hearty soups and stews.

Asparagus

There are three main types of asparagus: white, purple, and green. The fat, mildly flavored, white type is harvested as soon as the shoots start to poke through the soil. Purple and green asparagus are left to grow taller. The purple is tastier than the white, while the green type has the most pronounced flavor. Snap off the inedible woody end before briefly steaming, boiling, grillling, or roasting.

Carrot and beet

When buying carrots and beets, remember that the smaller ones are sweeter. Raw carrots and beets can be grated into salads or used to make relishes. Roasting them intensifies their sweetness and both work well in soups.

Celeriac

Celeriac, sometimes also called celery root, is a knobbly root with a flavor reminiscent of celery. Peel and grate raw into salads, or steam or bake; you can mix with potatoes to make a delicious mashed vegetable combination.

Celery

Celery lends a crunchy texture to salads and also makes a good base for soups and stews. Green celery is available all year round, and white is available in winter. Choose stems that are firm and rigid, but don't forget the leaves, which have a tangy flavor and can be added to stocks. Celery hearts can also be braised.

Fennel

Fennel has a mild anise seed flavor, which is most potent when eaten raw—thinly sliced in a salad, for example. Roasting fennel (cut into wedges) tempers the flavor and adds a delicious sweetness. Fennel also goes well with many traditional Mediterranean flavors, such as tomatoes, olive oil, garlic, and basil.

Globe artichoke

The distinguished globe artichoke has an exquisite flavor and is a lot of fun to eat: simply boil the heads, remove the hairy choke, then detach each leaf and dip into garlic butter, mayonnaise, or a vinaigrette dressing. The tastiest part is the fleshy base below the leaves. Cut it up and eat using a knife and fork.

Jerusalem artichoke

This small, knobbly tuber has a mild, nutty flavor and is delicious roasted, fried, or transformed into soup. Scrub instead of peel before use.

Potato

There are hundreds of potato varieties with different textures, which lend themselves to particular cooking methods. Waxy potatoes, such as round white or round red potatoes, are very good for serving boiled or in salads, while starchy varieties, such as russets, lend themselves to roasting, baking, and mashing.

Radish

Most well-known are the small radishes with red-skin, but there are other varieties, including the large black-skin radish and the more mildly flavored white daikon, or mooli. With their crisp peppery flesh, radishes are delicious added to salads, or dipped in sea salt flakes and eaten on their own as a snack.

Sweet potato

These torpedo-shape tubers have an orange or white flesh (the former is richer in beta carotene). When cooked, the white-flesh type has a drier texture, but both are good roasted, mashed, or baked.

Asparagus with Lemon Butter Sauce

Serves 4

ingredients
- 1 lb 12 oz/800 g asparagus spears, trimmed
- 1 tbsp olive oil
- salt and pepper

sauce
- juice of ½ lemon
- 2 tbsp water
- scant ½ cup butter, diced
- pepper

1 Preheat the oven to 400°F/200°C.

2 Lay the asparagus spears out in a single layer on a large baking sheet. Drizzle with the oil, season to taste with salt and pepper, and roast in the preheated oven for 10 minutes, or until just tender.

3 Meanwhile, make the sauce. Pour the lemon juice into a saucepan and add the water. Heat for a minute or so, then slowly add the butter, a little at a time, stirring continuously, until it has all been incorporated. Season to taste with pepper and serve immediately with the asparagus.

Asparagus & Sun-Dried
Tomato Risotto

Serves 4

ingredients

- 4 cups vegetable stock
- 1 tbsp olive oil
- 3 tbsp butter
- 1 small onion, finely chopped
- 6 sun-dried tomatoes, thinly sliced
- 1½ cups risotto rice
- ⅔ cup dry white wine
- 8 oz/225 g fresh asparagus spears, cooked
- ¾ cup grated Parmesan cheese, plus extra to garnish
- salt and pepper
- grated lemon rind, to garnish

1 Bring the stock to a boil in a saucepan, then reduce the heat and keep simmering gently over low heat while you are cooking the risotto.

2 Heat the oil with 2 tablespoons of the butter in a deep saucepan over medium heat until the butter has melted.

3 Stir in the onion and sun-dried tomatoes and cook, stirring occasionally, for 5 minutes, until the onion is soft and starting to turn golden. Do not brown.

4 Reduce the heat, add the rice, and mix to coat in oil and butter. Cook, stirring continuously, for 2–3 minutes, or until the grains are translucent. Add the wine and cook, stirring continuously, until it has reduced.

5 Gradually add the hot stock, a ladleful at a time. Stir continuously and add more liquid as the rice absorbs each addition. Increase the heat to medium so that the liquid simmers. Cook for 20 minutes, or until all the liquid is absorbed and the rice is creamy but still firm to the bite.

6 While the risotto is cooking, cut most of the asparagus into pieces about 1 inch/2.5 cm long. Set aside several asparagus tips for garnishing the finished dish. Carefully fold the remaining asparagus into the risotto for the last 5 minutes of cooking time.

7 Remove the risotto from the heat and add the remaining butter. Mix well, then stir in the Parmesan until it melts. Season to taste with salt and pepper. Spoon the risotto into individual warm serving dishes and garnish with reserved asparagus tips. Sprinkle some Parmesan and lemon rind on top and serve.

Baked Celery with Cream

Serves 4

ingredients
- 1 head celery
- ½ tsp ground cumin
- ½ tsp ground coriander
- 1 garlic clove, crushed
- 1 red onion, thinly sliced
- ½ cup halved pecans
- ⅔ cup vegetable stock
- ⅔ cup light cream
- 1 cup fresh whole wheat breadcrumbs
- ¼ cup grated Parmesan cheese
- salt and pepper

1 Preheat the oven to 400°F/200°C. Trim the celery and cut into matchsticks. Place the celery in an ovenproof dish with the cumin, coriander, garlic, onion, and pecans.

2 Mix the stock and cream together in a pitcher and pour over the vegetables. Season to taste with salt and pepper. Mix the breadcrumbs and cheese together in a small bowl and sprinkle over the top to cover the vegetables.

3 Cook in the preheated oven for 40 minutes, or until the vegetables are tender and the top is crispy. Serve immediately.

Globe Artichokes with Chive Mayonnaise

Serves 4

ingredients
- 4 globe artichokes
- 1 lemon, halved
- 2 eggs
- 2 egg yolks
- ¼ tsp dry mustard
- 1 cup sunflower oil
- ¼ cup snipped fresh chives, plus a few longer pieces to garnish
- salt and pepper

1 Using a very sharp knife, slice the stems and tips from the artichokes. Rub the cut surfaces with a lemon half to prevent blackening. Trim the tips of the remaining leaves with scissors and rub with the lemon half. Place the artichokes in a bowl of water to which you have added the juice of one of the lemon halves. Set aside the remaining lemon half.

2 Bring a saucepan of water to a boil. Add the artichokes, weighing them down with a heatproof plate to keep them submerged. Bring back to a boil, then boil for 30–40 minutes. Drain and place upside down on a plate to cool.

3 Meanwhile, put the whole eggs in a small saucepan and cover with cold water. Bring to a boil, and boil for 5 minutes. Drain and let cool. Peel the shells from the cooked eggs and slice in half lengthwise. Separate the yolks from the whites and put them in a mixing bowl with the raw egg yolks.

4 Beat the yolks for 1 minute, until smooth and sticky. Beat in the mustard, a pinch of salt, and a teaspoon of juice from the reserved lemon half. Add the oil, drop by drop, beating with each addition. Once the mixture starts to thicken, add the oil in a continuous thin stream, beating continuously. Thin with a little more lemon juice when all the oil is used up. Stir in the snipped chives and season with salt and pepper. Add more lemon juice, if necessary.

5 Using a pointed teaspoon, scoop out the hairy "choke" from the middle of the artichokes. To serve, place the artichokes on individual plates with the sauce to one side. Garnish with 2–3 long pieces of chive.

Jerusalem Artichoke Soup

Serves 4–6

ingredients
- 4 tbsp butter
- 2 onions, chopped
- 1 lb 8 oz/675 g Jerusalem artichokes, peeled and sliced
- 3½ cups vegetable stock
- 1¼ cups milk
- salt and pepper

croutons
- 2 slices day-old white bread, crusts removed
- 4 tbsp vegetable oil

1 To make the croutons, cut the bread into ½-inch/1-cm cubes. Heat the oil in a skillet and fry the croutons in a single layer, tossing occasionally, until they are golden brown and crisp. Remove the pan from the heat and spoon out the croutons onto paper towels to drain.

2 Melt the butter in a large saucepan over medium heat, add the onions, and cook until soft.

3 Add the Jerusalem artichokes and mix well with the butter, cover the saucepan, and cook slowly over low heat for about 10 minutes. Pour in the stock, bring to a boil, then reduce the heat and simmer, covered, for 20 minutes.

4 Remove from the heat and puree the soup in the saucepan using a handheld immersion blender, if you have one. Alternatively, pour into a blender, in batches if necessary, process until smooth, and return to the rinsed-out saucepan. Stir in the milk and season to taste with salt and pepper.

5 Heat the soup until hot, ladle into warm bowls, and serve with the crispy croutons.

Fennel Fritters with Red Bell Pepper Mayonnaise

Serves 6

ingredients

- 3 fennel bulbs, trimmed
- 1 cup dried white breadcrumbs
- 1 cup finely grated Parmesan cheese
- 2 tsp fennel seeds (optional)
- 1 egg, beaten
- sunflower oil, for shallow-frying
- salt and pepper
- lemon wedges, to serve

red bell pepper mayonnaise

- 2 red bell peppers
- 1 egg
- 1 tsp Dijon mustard
- 2–3 tbsp white wine vinegar
- pinch of salt
- 1¼ cups sunflower oil
- 2 fresh red chiles, seeded and chopped
- pepper

1 First make the mayonnaise. Using tongs, carefully hold each red bell pepper in turn over a high gas flame, turning frequently, for 8–10 minutes, or until blackened all over. Alternatively, preheat the oven to 425°F/ 220°C. Put the bell peppers on a baking sheet and cook in the preheated oven, turning frequently, for 10–15 minutes, or until blackened all over.

2 Put the bell peppers in a plastic bag, seal, and let cool. Peel off the charred skins and remove the seeds.

3 Put the egg, mustard, vinegar, and salt in a blender and process to combine. With the motor running, slowly trickle in about one-third of the oil. Once the mixture starts to thicken, add the remaining oil more quickly. When all the oil is incorporated, add the chiles and roasted bell peppers and process until smooth. Season to taste with pepper, then cover and chill in the refrigerator until required.

4 Cook the fennel bulbs in a large saucepan of salted boiling water for 15 minutes, or until almost tender—the exact cooking time will depend on their size. Drain and let cool, then carefully slice.

5 Mix the breadcrumbs and Parmesan cheese together, stir in the fennel seeds, if using, and season to taste with salt and pepper. Transfer the breadcrumb mixture to a large plate. Put the egg in a shallow dish. Coat the fennel slices in the egg and press the breadcrumb mixture firmly onto both sides.

6 Cover the bottom of a large skillet with oil to a depth of about ½ inch/1 cm. Heat over medium heat, add the fennel slices, and cook, turning once, until golden brown. Remove and drain on paper towels. Serve immediately with the red bell pepper mayonnaise along with lemon wedges to squeeze over.

Potato & Fennel Casserole

Serves 6

ingredients
- 9 potatoes (about 2 lb 4 oz/1 kg)
- 2–3 fennel bulbs
- 4 tbsp olive oil
- 1 onion, finely chopped
- 2 garlic cloves, crushed
- 4 fresh sage leaves
- ⅔ cup dry white wine
- salt and pepper

1 Preheat the oven to 400°F/200°C. Peel and finely slice the potatoes. Trim and finely slice the fennel.

2 Brush a large ovenproof dish with half of the oil. Layer half of the potato slices in the bottom of the prepared dish and season well with salt and pepper. Scatter half of the onion and garlic over the top and cover with the fennel. Scatter the remaining onion and garlic over the top and season to taste again with salt and pepper. Tuck the sage leaves into the vegetables. Finish with a neat layer of the potato slices and season to taste again with salt and pepper.

3 Pour in the wine and drizzle with the remaining oil. Cover the dish with foil and bake in the preheated oven for 30 minutes.

4 Remove the foil and bake for another 20–30 minutes, until the potatoes are brown and crisp.

Beet Salad

Serves 4–6

ingredients
- 2 lb/900 g beets
- 4 tbsp extra virgin olive oil
- 1½ tbsp red wine vinegar
- 2 garlic cloves, finely chopped
- 2 scallions, finely chopped
- salt

1 Carefully remove the roots from the beets without cutting into the skin, then cut off all but 1 inch/2.5 cm of the stems. Gently rub the beets under cold running water, without splitting the skins, to remove any dirt.

2 Put the beets in a saucepan with water to cover and bring to a boil. Cover, reduce the heat slightly, and cook for 25–40 minutes, depending on the size, until the largest beet is tender when pierced with a skewer or knife.

3 Meanwhile, put the oil, vinegar, garlic, scallions, and salt to taste in a jar with a screw-top lid and shake until emulsified, then set aside.

4 Drain the beets and rinse under cold running water until cool enough to handle, then peel away the skins. Thickly chop or slice the beets, then put in a bowl and pour in the dressing. Cover and chill in the refrigerator for at least 1 hour.

5 To serve, gently toss the salad and transfer to a serving bowl.

Borscht

Serves 6

ingredients

- 1 onion
- 4 tbsp butter
- 12 oz/350 g beets,
  cut into thin sticks, and
  1 beet, grated
- 1 carrot, cut into thin sticks
- 3 celery stalks, thinly sliced
- 2 tomatoes, peeled,
  seeded, and chopped
- 6 cups vegetable stock
- 1 tbsp white wine vinegar
- 1 tbsp sugar
- 2 tbsp snipped fresh dill
- 1¼ cups shredded white
  cabbage
- ⅔ cup sour cream
- salt and pepper
- crusty bread, to serve

1 Slice the onion into rings. Melt the butter in a large heavy-bottom saucepan. Add the onion and cook over low heat, stirring occasionally, for 3–5 minutes, or until softened. Add the beet sticks, carrot, celery, and tomatoes and cook, stirring frequently, for 4–5 minutes.

2 Add the stock, vinegar, sugar, and 1 tablespoon of the dill into the saucepan. Season to taste with salt and pepper. Bring to a boil, reduce the heat, and simmer for 35–40 minutes, or until the vegetables are tender.

3 Stir in the cabbage, cover, and simmer for 10 minutes. Stir in the grated beet with any juices and cook for an additional 10 minutes. Ladle into warm bowls. Top with the sour cream, sprinkle with the remaining dill, and serve with crusty bread.

Sweet Potato Ravioli with Sage Butter

Serves 4

ingredients
- 3¼ cups type 00 Italian pasta flour or all-purpose flour
- 4 eggs, beaten
- semolina, for dusting
- salt

filling
- 1 lb 2 oz/500 g sweet potatoes
- 3 tbsp olive oil
- 1 large onion, finely chopped
- 1 garlic clove, crushed
- 1 tsp chopped fresh thyme
- 2 tbsp honey
- salt and pepper

sage butter
- 3½ tbsp butter
- 1 bunch fresh sage leaves, finely chopped, plus extra leaves to garnish

1 To make the pasta dough, sift the flour into a large bowl or food processor. Add the eggs and bring the mixture together or process to make a soft but not sticky dough. Turn out onto a work surface lightly dusted with semolina and knead for 4–5 minutes, until smooth. Cover with plastic wrap and chill in the refrigerator for at least 30 minutes.

2 For the filling, peel the sweet potatoes and cut into chunks. Cook in a saucepan of boiling water for 20 minutes, or until tender. Drain and mash.

3 Heat the oil in a skillet over medium heat, add the onion, and cook, stirring frequently, for 4–5 minutes, until softened but not colored. Stir the onion into the mashed potatoes and add the garlic and thyme. Drizzle with the honey and season to taste with salt and pepper. Set aside.

4 Using a pasta machine, roll the pasta out to a thickness of about ¹⁄₃₂ inch/ 1 mm (or use a rolling pin on a work surface lightly dusted with semolina).

5 Cut the pasta in half. Place teaspoonfuls of the filling at evenly spaced intervals across half of the pasta. Brush around the filling with a small amount of water and cover with the second half of the pasta. Press lightly around the filling to seal, and cut into squares with a sharp knife or pastry wheel. Lay the ravioli out on a sheet of wax paper that has been lightly dusted with semolina.

6 Bring a large saucepan of salted water to a boil and drop in the ravioli. Cook for 2–3 minutes, until the pasta rises to the surface and is tender but still firm to the bite.

7 Meanwhile, for the sage butter, melt the butter with the chopped sage in a small saucepan over low heat.

8 Drain the ravioli and immediately toss with the sage butter. Serve immediately, garnished with sage leaves.

Roasted Potato Wedges
with Shallots & Rosemary

Serves 4

ingredients
- 2 lb 4 oz/1 kg small potatoes
- 6 tbsp olive oil
- 2 fresh rosemary sprigs
- 5½ oz/150 g baby shallots
- 2 garlic cloves, sliced
- salt and pepper

1 Preheat the oven to 400°F/200°C. Peel and cut each potato into 8 thick wedges. Put the potatoes in a large saucepan of lightly salted water and bring to a boil. Reduce the heat and simmer for 5 minutes.

2 Heat the oil in a large roasting pan on the stove. Drain the potatoes well and add to the roasting pan. Strip the leaves from the rosemary sprigs, chop finely, and sprinkle over the potatoes.

3 Roast the potatoes in the preheated oven for 35 minutes, turning twice during cooking. Add the shallots and garlic and roast for an additional 15 minutes, until golden brown. Season to taste with salt and pepper.

4 Transfer to a warm serving dish and serve immediately.

Cabbage & Mashed Potatoes

Serves 3–4

ingredients

- ½ small head green or white cabbage
- 6 scallions, cut into ¼-inch/5-mm slices
- salt and pepper

mashed potatoes

- 4 starchy potatoes, such as russets, cut into chunks
- 4 tbsp butter
- ⅔ cup light cream
- salt and pepper

1 To make the mashed potatoes, cook the potatoes in a large saucepan of boiling salted water for 15–20 minutes. Drain well and mash with a potato masher until smooth. Season to taste with salt and pepper, add the butter and cream, and stir well. The potato should be very soft.

2 Meanwhile, cut the cabbage into quarters, remove and discard the stem in the center, and shred the leaves finely.

3 Cook the cabbage in a large saucepan of boiling salted water for 1–2 minutes, until soft. Drain thoroughly.

4 Mix the potato and cabbage together and stir in the scallions. Season well with salt and pepper. Serve immediately.

Potato Fritters with Onion & Tomato Relish

Serves 8

ingredients

- ½ cup whole wheat flour
- ½ tsp ground coriander
- ½ tsp cumin seeds
- ¼ tsp chili powder
- ½ tsp turmeric
- ¼ tsp salt
- 1 egg
- 3 tbsp milk
- 3 potatoes
- 1–2 garlic cloves, crushed
- 4 scallions, chopped
- ⅓ cup corn kernels
- vegetable oil, for shallow-frying

onion & tomato relish

- 1 onion
- 2 tomatoes
- 2 tbsp chopped fresh cilantro
- 2 tbsp chopped fresh mint
- 2 tbsp lemon juice
- ½ tsp roasted cumin seeds
- ¼ tsp salt
- pinch of cayenne pepper

1 First make the relish. Cut the onion and tomatoes into small dice and place in a bowl with the remaining ingredients. Mix together well and let stand for at least 15 minutes before serving to let the flavors blend.

2 Place the flour in a bowl, stir in the spices and salt, and make a well in the center. Add the egg and milk and mix to form a fairly thick batter.

3 Coarsely grate the potatoes, place them in a strainer, and rinse well under cold running water. Drain and squeeze dry, then stir them into the batter with the garlic, scallions, and corn kernels and mix to combine thoroughly.

4 Heat about ¼ inch/5 mm of oil in a large skillet and add a few tablespoons of the mixture at a time, flattening each to form a thin cake. Fry over low heat, turning frequently, for 2–3 minutes, or until golden brown and cooked through.

5 Drain the fritters on paper towels and keep them hot while frying the remaining mixture in the same way. Serve the potato fritters hot with the relish.

Celeriac Soup with Cheese Pastry Sticks

Serves 4

ingredients
- 3 tbsp olive oil
- 1 onion, chopped
- 1 celeriac, peeled and cut into chunks
- 4 cups vegetable stock
- 1 small bunch fresh thyme, chopped, plus extra sprigs to garnish
- salt and pepper

cheese pastry sticks
- butter, for greasing
- 13 oz/375 g prepared puff pastry, thawed if frozen
- all-purpose flour, for dusting
- 1 egg, beaten
- 1 cup finely grated Parmesan cheese
- pepper

1 Heat the oil in a large saucepan over medium heat, add the onion, and cook, stirring frequently, for 4–5 minutes, until softened but not colored. Add the celeriac and cook, stirring frequently, for 3–4 minutes. Pour in the stock and add the chopped thyme. Simmer for 25 minutes, or until the celeriac is tender.

2 Meanwhile, preheat the oven to 400°F/200°C. Lightly grease two baking sheets.

3 For the pastry sticks, roll the pastry out thinly on a floured work surface. Brush with half of the egg and scatter half of the Parmesan cheese over the top. Add a good grinding of pepper. Fold the pastry in half. Brush with the remaining egg, scatter with the remaining cheese, and add another grinding of pepper. Cut into strips about ½ inch/1 cm wide, then twist the pastry strips gently along their length to produce spiral shapes.

4 Place the pastry strips onto the prepared baking sheets. Bake in the preheated oven for 5 minutes, or until crisp and golden.

5 Remove the celeriac mixture from the heat and puree the soup in the saucepan using a handheld immersion blender, if you have one. Alternatively, pour into a blender, in batches if necessary, process until smooth, and return to the rinsed-out saucepan. Season to taste with salt and pepper.

6 Ladle the soup into warm bowls and garnish with thyme sprigs. Serve with the warm pastry sticks.

Carrot & Orange Stir-Fry

Serves 4

ingredients

- 2 tbsp sunflower oil
- 4 cups grated carrots
- 2–3 leeks (about 8 oz/225 g), shredded
- 2 oranges, peeled and segmented
- 2 tbsp ketchup
- 1 tbsp Demerara sugar or raw brown sugar
- 2 tbsp light soy sauce
- ⅔ cup chopped peanuts

1 Heat the oil in a large wok. Add the carrots and leeks to the wok and stir-fry for 2–3 minutes, or until the vegetables are just soft.

2 Add the oranges to the wok and heat through gently, making sure that you do not break up the orange segments as you stir the mixture.

3 Mix the ketchup, sugar, and soy sauce together in a small bowl.

4 Add the ketchup mixture to the wok and stir-fry for an additional 2 minutes.

5 Transfer the stir-fry to warm serving bowls and scatter the peanuts over the top. Serve immediately.

Carrot Upside-Down Tart

Serves 4

ingredients
- 1 lb 5 oz/600 g young carrots, cut into 1-inch/2.5-cm chunks
- 2 tbsp honey
- 3½ tbsp butter
- 1 small bunch fresh thyme, chopped
- 12 oz/350 g ready-made puff pastry, thawed if frozen
- all-purpose flour, for dusting
- salt and pepper

1 Preheat the oven to 400°F/200°C.

2 Cook the carrots in a saucepan of boiling water for 10–15 minutes, until just tender. Drain, toss with the honey, butter, and thyme, and season to taste with salt and pepper. Spoon over the bottom of an 8-inch/20-cm tart pan or round cake pan with a depth of about 1¼ inches/3 cm and roast in the preheated oven for 15 minutes, or until the carrots are caramelized.

3 Roll the pastry out onto a floured work surface into a round large enough to fit the pan and with an extra ¾-inch/2-cm edge. Lay the pastry carefully over the carrots and tuck the edge down between the carrots and the side of the pan to make a border. Bake in the oven for 15 minutes, or until the pastry is puffed and golden.

4 Remove the pan from the oven and turn out upside down onto a plate. Serve immediately.

Roasted Root Vegetables

Serves 4–6

ingredients

- 3 parsnips, cut into 2-inch/5-cm chunks
- 4 baby turnips, cut into quarters
- 3 carrots, cut into 2-inch/5-cm chunks
- ½ butternut squash, peeled and cut into 2-inch/5-cm chunks
- 1 lb/450 g sweet potatoes, peeled and cut into 2-inch/5-cm chunks
- 2 garlic cloves, finely chopped
- 2 tbsp chopped fresh rosemary
- 2 tbsp chopped fresh thyme
- 2 tsp chopped fresh sage
- 3 tbsp olive oil
- salt and pepper
- 2 tbsp chopped fresh mixed herbs, such as parsley, thyme, and mint, to garnish

1 Preheat the oven to 425°F/220°C.

2 Arrange all the vegetables in a single layer in a large roasting pan. Scatter the garlic, rosemary, thyme, and sage over the top. Pour in the oil and season well with salt and pepper.

3 Toss all the ingredients together until they are well mixed and coated with the oil (you can let them marinate at this stage to let the flavors be absorbed).

4 Roast the vegetables at the top of the preheated oven for 50–60 minutes, until they are cooked and nicely browned. Turn the vegetables over halfway through the cooking time. Serve immediately, garnished with the mixed herbs.

Chapter 3
Brassicas & Leafy Greens

Directory of Brassicas & Leafy Greens

Brassicas, or the cabbage family, includes broccoli, Brussels sprouts, and cauliflower. Some brassicas are also considered leafy greens, such as spinach and kale. Other types of leafy greens include arugula, radicchio, and watercress.

Arugula and watercress

Both arugula and watercress have a distinctive, peppery flavor and will enliven any salad. They are milder when cooked, but will still retain some bite. They make delicious soups and sauces, and can be stirred into pasta or risotto.

Belgian endive and radicchio

The elongated, tightly packed leaves of Belgian endive and the firm, round heads of radicchio have a bitter taste, so use sparingly in salads. Both are good broiled, sautéed, or braised, which mellow the flavor.

Bok choy

Bok choy has densely packed, dark green leaves with a white, fleshy base. It has a mild flavor, and makes a delightful addition to stir-fries, soups, noodle dishes, and salads. For stir-frying, it's best to cut the green leafy part from the base because the base takes longer to cook.

Broccoli

The type of broccoli generally found in supermarkets has a broad, tightly budded head divided into florets and a thick central stem. Thinly sliced, the stem can be lightly steamed with the florets or served raw as a crudité. Baby broccoli is not necessarily young broccoli, but may refer to Broccolini, a cross between broccoli and Chinese broccoli. It is similar to broccoli, but with thinner stems and a flavor that is a cross between broccoli and asparagus.

Brussels sprouts

Reminiscent of Christmas, Brussels sprouts are like miniature cabbages and have a strong, nutty flavor. They are best cooked very lightly, either steamed or stir-fried.

Cabbage

When lightly cooked or served shredded in a salad, cabbage is delicious. Varieties range from the crinkly leaved savoy, which is ideal for stuffing, to the smooth, firm, white and red types. Chinese cabbage has a more delicate flavor and is best used in salads or stir-fries.

Cauliflower

Cauliflower comes in many varieties, ranging from white to pale green and purple. Cauliflower is cooked in the same way as broccoli. It has an understated flavor, which is enhanced by creamy sauces or melted cheese. It is also good in curries.

Endive and escarole

These are both a type of chicory. Escarole has broad, flat leaves, while curly endive or frisée has frilly leaves. Both have a mild flavor with only a hint of bitterness.

Kale and collard greens

Kale has curly edged, long-stemmed leaves attached to a central stalk. Collard greens are similar but with larger, smoother leaves. Both are full of flavor and packed with nutrients. They are best steamed or lightly boiled. The young leaves can be used in stir-fries or raw in salads.

Lettuce

Roman and iceberg have firm, crisp leaves, while Boston is softer and sweeter. Looseleaf lettuce don't form a head and the leaves can be smooth or frilly. One attractive type is the dark red oak leaf lettuce. Lettuce aren't just for salads; they are also good braised or turned into flavorsome soups.

Spinach

One of the most versatile leafy greens, spinach has a rich, buttery flavor and smooth texture. It's best either lightly boiled or steamed, or quickly sautéed in butter. Spinach is also good added to a risotto or pasta dish. Eaten raw, the young leaves make a highly nutritious addition to a salad.

Swiss chard

Swiss chard has dark green, crinkled leaves and a broad white, yellow, pink, or red stem. The stem takes longer to cook than the leaves, so it is best sliced and cooked slightly before the leaves are added.

Broccoli & Cheddar Soup

Serves 6

ingredients
- 2 tbsp butter
- 1 onion, chopped
- 2 tsp chopped fresh tarragon, plus extra to garnish
- 3 cups grated potatoes,
- 7¼ cups vegetable stock
- 1 bunch broccoli, cut into small florets
- 1½ cups grated cheddar cheese
- 1 tbsp chopped fresh parsley
- salt and pepper

1 Melt the butter in a large heavy-bottom saucepan. Add the onion and cook, stirring occasionally, for 5 minutes, until soft. Add the tarragon to the saucepan with the potatoes, season to taste with salt and pepper, and mix well. Pour in just enough of the stock to cover and bring to a boil. Reduce the heat, cover, and simmer for 10 minutes.

2 Meanwhile, bring the remaining stock to a boil in a separate saucepan. Add the broccoli and cook for 6–8 minutes, until just tender.

3 Remove both pans from the heat, let cool slightly, then ladle the contents of both into a blender or food processor, in batches if necessary. Process until smooth, then pour the mixture into a clean saucepan.

4 Stir the cheese into the pan with the parsley and heat gently to warm through, but do not let the soup boil. Ladle into warm soup bowls, garnish with tarragon, and serve immediately.

Broccoli & Wild Garlic
Crostini

Serves 6

ingredients

- 1 bunch broccoli, cut into small florets
- scant ½ cup olive oil
- 1 small bunch wild garlic, rinsed, patted dry, and chopped
- 1–2 fresh red chiles, seeded and finely chopped
- 6 slices country-style bread
- salt and pepper

1 Preheat the oven to 375°F/190°C.

2 Cook the broccoli in a large saucepan of boiling salted water for 10 minutes, or until just tender. Drain well and set aside.

3 Heat about one-third of the oil in a wok or large skillet over high heat, add the wild garlic and the chile, and stir-fry for 2 minutes. Add the broccoli, season to taste with salt and pepper, and stir-fry for 3–4 minutes, until hot and crisp.

4 Meanwhile, drizzle the remaining oil evenly over the bread slices and bake in the preheated oven for 10 minutes, or until crisp and golden.

5 Divide the broccoli mixture among the crostini, season to taste with pepper, and serve immediately.

Chile Broccoli Pasta

Serves 4

ingredients
- 8 oz/225 g dried tortiglioni
- ½ bunch broccoli
- 4 tbsp extra virgin olive oil
- 2 large garlic cloves, chopped
- 2 fresh red chiles, seeded and diced
- 8 cherry tomatoes, halved if large (optional)
- salt
- small handful chopped fresh basil or parsley, to garnish

1 Bring a large saucepan of lightly salted water to a boil. Add the pasta, return to a boil, and cook for 8–10 minutes, or according to the package directions, until the pasta is tender but still firm to the bite. Remove from the heat, drain, rinse with cold water, and drain again. Set aside.

2 Cut the broccoli into florets. Bring a saucepan of lightly salted water to a boil, add the broccoli, and cook for 5 minutes. Drain, rinse with cold water, and drain again.

3 Heat the oil in the pan that the pasta was cooked in. Add the garlic, chiles, and tomatoes, if using. Cook over high heat for 1 minute.

4 Return the broccoli to the pan and mix well. Cook for 2 minutes to heat through. Add the pasta and mix well again. Cook for an additional minute.

5 Remove the pasta from the heat, turn into a large serving bowl, and serve, garnished with basil.

Cauliflower & Broccoli Tart

Serves 4

ingredients

pie dough
- heaping 1⅓ cups all-purpose flour, plus extra for dusting
- pinch of salt
- 1¼ tsp paprika
- 1 tsp dried thyme
- 5½ tbsp margarine
- 3 tbsp water

filling
- 1 cup cauliflower florets
- 1½ cups broccoli florets
- 1 onion, cut into 8 wedges
- 2 tbsp butter or margarine
- 1 tbsp all-purpose flour
- generous ⅓ cup vegetable stock
- ½ cup milk
- ¾ cup grated cheddar cheese
- salt and pepper
- paprika, to garnish

1 Preheat the oven to 375°F/190°C. To make the pie dough, sift the flour and salt into a bowl. Add the paprika and thyme and rub in the margarine. Stir in the water and bind to form a dough. Let chill in the refrigerator for 30 minutes.

2 Roll out the dough on a floured work surface and use to line a 7-inch/18-cm loose-bottom tart pan. Prick the bottom with a fork and line with parchment paper. Fill with pie weights or dried beans and bake in the preheated oven for 15 minutes. Remove the paper and weights and return the pastry shell to the oven for 5 minutes.

3 To make the filling, bring a large saucepan of lightly salted water to a boil, add the cauliflower, broccoli, and onion, and cook for 10–12 minutes, until tender. Drain and reserve.

4 Melt the butter in a saucepan. Add the flour and cook, stirring continuously, for 1 minute. Remove from the heat, stir in the stock and milk, and return to the heat. Bring to a boil, stirring continuously, and add ½ cup of the cheese. Season to taste with salt and pepper.

5 Spoon the cauliflower, broccoli, and onion into the pastry shell. Pour the sauce over the top and sprinkle with the remaining cheese. Return the tart to the oven and bake for 10 minutes, until the cheese is golden and bubbling. Garnish with paprika and serve immediately.

Cauliflower, Eggplant & Green Bean Korma

Serves 4–6

ingredients

- ¾ cup cashew nuts
- 1½ tbsp garlic and ginger paste
- scant 1 cup water, plus extra if needed
- 4 tbsp ghee, vegetable oil, or peanut oil
- 1 large onion, chopped
- 5 green cardamom pods, lightly crushed
- 1 cinnamon stick, broken in half
- ¼ tsp ground turmeric
- generous 1 cup heavy cream
- 5 oz/140 g new potatoes, scrubbed and chopped into ½-inch/1-cm pieces
- 1 cup cauliflower florets
- ½ tsp garam masala
- 1¾ cups eggplant chunks
- 1¼ cups ½-inch/1-cm green bean pieces
- salt and pepper
- chopped fresh mint or cilantro, to garnish

1 Heat a large flameproof casserole or skillet with a tight-fitting lid over high heat. Add the nuts and stir until they start to brown, then turn them out of the casserole.

2 Put the nuts in a spice blender with the garlic and ginger paste and 1 tablespoon of the water and process until a coarse paste forms.

3 Melt the ghee in the casserole over medium–high heat. Add the onion and fry for 5–8 minutes, or until golden brown. Add the nut paste and stir for 5 minutes. Stir in the cardamom pods, cinnamon stick, and turmeric. Add the cream and the remaining water and bring to a boil, stirring. Reduce the heat to the lowest level, cover the casserole, and simmer for 5 minutes.

4 Add the potatoes, cauliflower, and garam masala to the casserole and simmer, covered, for 5 minutes. Stir in the eggplant and green beans and continue simmering for an additional 5 minutes, or until all the vegetables are tender. Check the sauce occasionally to make sure it isn't sticking to the bottom of the casserole, and stir in extra water, if needed.

5 Taste and adjust the seasoning, adding salt and pepper if needed. Sprinkle with mint and serve.

Cauliflower With Cheese

Serves 4

ingredients
- 1 cauliflower, trimmed and cut into florets
- 3 tbsp butter
- ⅓ cup all-purpose flour
- 2 cups milk
- 1 cup finely grated cheddar cheese
- freshly grated nutmeg
- salt and pepper
- 1 tbsp grated Parmesan cheese

1 Preheat the broiler to high. Cook the cauliflower in a saucepan of boiling salted water for 4–5 minutes. It should still be firm. Drain, place in a hot 6-cup gratin dish and keep warm.

2 Melt the butter in the rinsed-out saucepan over medium heat and stir in the flour. Cook, stirring continuously, for 1 minute, until smooth.

3 Remove from the heat and gradually stir in the milk until you have a smooth consistency.

4 Return to low heat and continue to stir while the sauce comes to a boil and thickens. Reduce the heat and simmer gently, stirring continuously, for about 3 minutes, until the sauce is creamy and smooth.

5 Remove from the heat and stir in the cheddar cheese and nutmeg to taste. Taste and season well with salt and pepper.

6 Pour the hot sauce over the cauliflower, top with the Parmesan, and place under the preheated broiler to brown. Serve immediately.

Brussels Sprouts
with Chestnuts

Serves 4

ingredients

- 1 lb/450 g Brussels sprouts
- ½ cup unsalted butter
- ¼ cup brown sugar
- 6 oz/175 g chestnuts, shelled and cooked
- salt and pepper

1 Trim the sprouts, removing the coarse stems and any loose outer leaves. Bring a large saucepan of lightly salted water to the boil over high heat. Add the sprouts and boil for 5–10 minutes, until just cooked but not too soft. Drain well, rinse in cold water, and drain again. Set aside.

2 Melt the butter in a heavy-bottom skillet. Add the sugar and stir over medium heat until dissolved.

3 Add the chestnuts to the skillet and cook, stirring occasionally, until they are well coated and starting to brown.

4 Add the sprouts to the skillet with the chestnuts and mix well. Reduce the heat and cook gently, stirring occasionally, for 3–4 minutes to heat through. Season to taste with salt and pepper.

5 Remove from the heat, transfer to a serving dish, and serve.

Traditional Tuscan
Bean & Cabbage Soup

Serves 6

ingredients
- 1 cup dried cannellini beans, soaked in cold water overnight
- 3 tbsp olive oil
- 2 red onions, coarsely chopped
- 4 carrots, sliced
- 4 celery stalks, coarsely chopped
- 4 garlic cloves, coarsely chopped
- 2½ cups water or vegetable stock
- 14 oz/400 g canned chopped tomatoes
- 2 tbsp chopped fresh flat-leaf parsley
- 1 lb 2 oz/500 g cavolo nero or black-leaf kale, trimmed and finely sliced
- 1 small 2-day-old ciabatta loaf, torn into small pieces
- salt and pepper
- extra virgin olive oil, to serve

1 Drain the beans and put in a large saucepan. Cover with fresh cold water and bring to a boil, skimming off any foam that rises to the surface. Reduce the heat and simmer, uncovered, for 1–1½ hours, until tender, adding more water if required.

2 Meanwhile, heat the olive oil in a large saucepan, add the onions, carrots, and celery, and cook over medium heat, stirring frequently, for 10–15 minutes, until soft. Add the garlic and cook, stirring, for 1–2 minutes.

3 Drain the beans, reserving the cooking water, and add half of the beans to the vegetable mixture. Pour in the measured water and the tomatoes, add the parsley, and season well with salt and pepper. Bring to a simmer and cook, uncovered and stirring occasionally, for 30 minutes. Add the cavolo nero and cook, stirring occasionally, for another 15 minutes.

4 Put the remaining beans in a food processor or blender with some of the reserved cooking water and process until smooth. Add to the soup. Stir in the bread. The soup should be thick, but add more of the reserved cooking water to thin, if necessary. Continue to cook until heated through.

5 Serve hot, drizzled with extra virgin olive oil.

Kale Stir-Fry

Serves 4

ingredients

- 1 lb 10 oz/750 g kale
- 2 tbsp sunflower oil
- 1 onion, chopped
- 4 large garlic cloves, finely chopped
- 2 red bell peppers, seeded and thinly sliced
- 1 large carrot, coarsely grated
- 1½ cup small broccoli florets
- pinch of dried chili flakes (optional)
- ½ cup vegetable stock
- 1 cup mixed bean sprouts
- handful of toasted cashew nuts, chopped
- salt and pepper
- lemon wedges, to serve

1 Using a sharp knife, cut out the thick central stems from the kale. Stack several leaves on top of each other, then cut across them to finely shred; repeat until all the kale is shredded. Set aside.

2 Heat a large wok with a lid over high heat until a splash of water "dances" on the surface. Add the oil and swirl it around. Add the onion and stir-fry for about 3 minutes, then add the garlic, bell peppers, and carrot and continue stir-frying until the onion is tender and the bell peppers are starting to soften.

3 Add the broccoli and chili flakes, if using, and stir. Add the kale to the wok and stir. Add the stock and salt and pepper to taste, reduce the heat to medium, cover the wok, and simmer for about 5 minutes, until the kale is tender.

4 Remove the lid and let any excess liquid evaporate. Use two forks to mix the bean sprouts through the other ingredients, then adjust the seasoning, adding salt and pepper, if needed.

5 Transfer to serving plates, scatter the nuts over the top, and serve with lemon wedges.

Stuffed Cabbage Rolls

Serves 4

ingredients

- 8 large or 12 medium green cabbage leaves
- 4 cups water
- ½ cup pearl barley, rinsed and drained
- 2 tbsp chopped fresh parsley
- 2 garlic cloves, coarsely chopped
- 1 lb 12 oz/800 g canned chopped tomatoes
- 4 tbsp red wine vinegar
- 1 tbsp sunflower or corn oil, plus extra for brushing
- 2 zucchini, diced
- 3 scallions, sliced
- 2 tbsp brown sugar
- salt and pepper

1 Cut out the thick central stems from the cabbage leaves. Bring a large saucepan of water to a boil, add the cabbage leaves, and blanch for 1 minute. Drain the leaves well and spread out to dry.

2 Bring the measured water to a boil in a large saucepan. Add the barley and half of the chopped parsley, cover, and simmer for about 45 minutes, until the liquid has been absorbed.

3 Meanwhile, put the garlic, half of the tomatoes, and the vinegar in a blender or food processor and process to a smooth puree. Scrape into a bowl and set aside.

4 Heat the oil in a large skillet. Add the zucchini and the remaining parsley and cook, stirring frequently, for 3 minutes. Add the scallions and cook briefly, then add the tomato mixture. Cook for 10 minutes, until thickened, then transfer to a large bowl.

5 Add the cooked barley to the bowl, season to taste with salt and pepper, and stir well.

6 Preheat the oven to 375°F/190°C. Lightly brush an ovenproof dish with oil. Place a spoonful of the barley mixture at the stem end of a cabbage leaf. Roll up, tucking in the sides, and place, seam-side down, in the dish. Stuff and roll the remaining cabbage leaves in the same way, placing them in the dish in a single layer.

7 Sprinkle the sugar over the cabbage rolls and pour the remaining tomatoes, with their can juices, on top. Cover with foil and bake in the preheated oven for 30 minutes, or until tender. Serve straight from the dish.

Red Curry with Mixed Leaves

Serves 4

ingredients

- 2 tbsp peanut or vegetable oil
- 2 onions, thinly sliced
- 1 bunch fine asparagus spears
- 14 fl oz/400 ml canned coconut milk
- 2 tbsp Thai red curry paste
- 3 fresh kaffir lime leaves
- 8 oz/225 g baby spinach leaves
- 2 heads bok choy, chopped
- 1 small head Chinese cabbage, shredded
- handful fresh cilantro, chopped
- cooked rice, to serve

1 Heat the oil in a wok, add the onions and asparagus, and stir-fry over medium–high heat for 1–2 minutes.

2 Add the coconut milk, curry paste, and lime leaves and bring gently to a boil, stirring occasionally.

3 Add the spinach, bok choy, and Chinese cabbage and cook, stirring, for 2–3 minutes, until wilted.

4 Add the cilantro and stir well. Serve immediately with rice.

Spinach & Ricotta Gnocchi

Serves 4–6

ingredients

- 1 tbsp olive oil
- 1 lb 2 oz/500 g spinach leaves
- 8 oz/225 g ricotta cheese
- 1 cup grated Parmesan or Pecorino Romano cheese
- 2 eggs, lightly beaten
- scant ½ cup all-purpose flour, plus extra for dusting
- freshly grated nutmeg
- salt and pepper
- fresh basil leaves, shredded, to garnish

sauce

- 2 tbsp olive oil
- 2 shallots, finely chopped
- 1 carrot, finely diced
- 2 garlic cloves, crushed
- 1 lb 12 oz/800 g canned chopped tomatoes
- 1 tbsp tomato paste
- 6 fresh basil leaves, coarsely torn into pieces
- salt and pepper

1 Heat the oil in a large saucepan. Add the spinach and cook, covered, for 1–2 minutes, until just wilted. Drain through a strainer and let cool, then squeeze out as much water as possible with your hands (you can squeeze it in a clean dish towel to make sure that it is very dry).

2 Finely chop the spinach and put in a bowl. Add the ricotta cheese, half of the Parmesan cheese, the eggs, and flour and mix well. Season to taste with salt, pepper, and nutmeg. Cover and chill in the refrigerator for at least 1 hour.

3 Meanwhile, make the sauce. Heat the oil in a saucepan, add the shallots, carrot, and garlic and cook over medium heat, stirring frequently, for 3–4 minutes, until soft. Add the tomatoes and tomato paste and bring to a boil, then reduce the heat and simmer, uncovered, for 10–15 minutes, until the sauce is reduced and thickened. Season to taste with salt and pepper and add the basil leaves. If you prefer a smooth sauce, pass it through a strainer or process in a food processor or blender.

4 Lightly dust a baking sheet with flour. To shape the gnocchi, flour a plate and your hands thoroughly. Put a small tablespoonful of the spinach mixture into the palm of one hand, roll gently into an egg shape, and transfer to the prepared baking sheet. Repeat with the remaining spinach mixture.

5 Bring a large saucepan of water to a simmer, carefully add the gnocchi, in small batches, and cook gently for 2–3 minutes, until they rise to the surface. Remove with a slotted spoon and transfer to a warm dish to keep warm while you cook the remaining gnocchi.

6 Transfer the gnocchi to individual serving dishes and pour the sauce over the top. Garnish with basil and serve immediately with the remaining Parmesan cheese.

Pasta with Honeyed
Belgian Endive & Walnuts

Serves 4

ingredients
- 3 tbsp olive oil
- 2 garlic cloves, crushed
- 3 heads Belgian endive, sliced
- 1 tbsp honey
- ¾ cup walnuts
- 1 lb/450 g dried penne
- salt and pepper

1 Heat the oil in a skillet over low heat, add the garlic and endive, and cook, stirring, for 3–4 minutes, until the endive begins to wilt. Stir in the honey and walnuts and cook, stirring occasionally, for another 4–5 minutes. Season to taste with salt and pepper.

2 Meanwhile, bring a large saucepan of lightly salted water to a boil. Add the pasta, return to a boil, and cook for 8–10 minutes, or according to the package directions, until the pasta is tender but still firm to the bite.

3 Drain the pasta and toss with the endive mixture. Serve immediately.

Watercress, Zucchini & Mint Salad

Serves 4

ingredients
- 2 zucchini, cut into thin sticks
- 1 cup short green bean pieces
- 1 green bell pepper, seeded and cut into strips
- 2 celery stalks, sliced
- 1 bunch watercress
- salt

dressing
- 1 cup plain yogurt
- 1 garlic clove, crushed
- 2 tbsp chopped fresh mint
- pepper

1 Bring a saucepan of lightly salted water to a boil, add the zucchini and beans, and cook for 7–8 minutes. Drain, rinse under cold running water, and drain again. Set aside to cool completely.

2 Mix the zucchini and beans with the green bell pepper, celery, and watercress in a large serving bowl.

3 To make the dressing, combine the yogurt, garlic, and mint in a small bowl. Season to taste with pepper.

4 Spoon the dressing onto the salad and serve immediately.

Spaghetti with Arugula &
Hazelnut Pesto

Serves 4

ingredients

- 2 garlic cloves
- ⅔ cup hazelnuts
- 5½ oz/150 g arugula, coarse stems removed
- 1 cup grated Parmesan cheese, plus extra to serve
- 6 tbsp extra virgin olive oil
- 4 oz/115 g mascarpone cheese
- 14 oz/400 g dried spaghetti
- salt and pepper

1 Put the garlic and hazelnuts in a food processor and process until finely chopped. Add the arugula, Parmesan, and oil and process until smooth and thoroughly combined. Scrape the pesto into a large serving dish, season to taste with salt and pepper, and stir in the mascarpone.

2 Bring a large saucepan of salted water to a boil. Add the pasta, return to a boil, and cook for 8–10 minutes, or according to the package directions, until tender but still firm to the bite.

3 Stir ½–⅔ cup of the pasta cooking water into the pesto, mixing well until thoroughly combined. Drain the pasta, add it to the dish, and toss well to coat. Sprinkle with Parmesan and serve immediately.

Radicchio & Red Bell Pepper Salad

Serves 4

ingredients
- 2 red bell peppers
- 1 head radicchio, separated into leaves
- 4 cooked whole beets, cut into matchsticks
- 12 radishes, sliced
- 4 scallons, finely chopped
- 4 tbsp prepared salad dressing
- crusty bread, to serve

1 Core and seed the red bell peppers and cut into rounds.

2 Arrange the radicchio leaves in a salad bowl. Add the peppers, beets, radishes, and scallions.

3 Drizzle with the dressing, toss well, and serve with crusty bread.

Chapter 4
Mushrooms & the Onion Family

Directory of Mushrooms & the Onion Family

Both mushrooms and the onion family have traditionally been used to provide the base for many dishes, although, as this chapter shows, they really come into their own when served as the star of many delicious main-course dishes.

Mushrooms

There is a wide range of mushrooms from which to choose, both fresh and dried, and many types of wild mushroom are now cultivated. They are extremely versatile and can be eaten raw in salads, cooked as a vegetable accompaniment, or used to flavor a variety of dishes ranging from soups to risottos.

Dried mushrooms keep well. To reconstitute them, soak in boiling water for 20–30 minutes. Drain and rinse well to remove any dirt and grit. You can use the soaking water in stocks and sauces, but strain first.

Chanterelle

Highly prized, golden chanterelles have a fruity, nutty flavor. They should be wiped clean instead of washed, because they are very porous. In fact, most types of mushrooms should be prepared in this way, apart from the honeycomb-capped morel.

Cremini and portabello

Creminis are intensely flavored, brown button mushrooms. They are a miniature version of the portabello—a large, flat, dense-fleshed mushroom with a meaty flavor.

Morel

Recognizable by its cone-shape honeycomb cap, wild morels make an appearance from April until June, but the cultivated version is available throughout the year, albeit sporadically. They have an open, porous texture and a mild, sweetish flavor. Dried morels have a more intense flavor.

Porcino

Also known as cèpes, porcini have a meaty texture and woody flavor. Dried porcini lend a rich flavor to soups, stocks, and sauces.

Shiitake and oyster

Both shiitake and oyster mushrooms are now widely cultivated. Oysters are fluted in shape, and are usually grayish-brown in color, though they also come in pale yellow and pink. The flavor is mild. In some regions, they can be found year round, and they are also available canned; the latter type should be rinsed before using. Shiitakes have a chewy texture and robust flavor, and are most commonly used in Asian dishes. Also known as the golden oak or the Chinese black mushroom, shiitakes are at their peak in spring and fall.

Onion family

Garlic, leeks, onions, and shallots provide substance and unifying flavor to all kinds of savory dishes, particularly those for vegetarians. They are also delicious cooked on their own.

Garlic

Amazingly versatile, garlic adds essential flavor to dishes from all over the world. Whole heads of garlic are also delicious roasted and served as a vegetable. Used raw, the crushed cloves can be mashed with butter for garnishing broiled meat, or added to mayonnaise to make aioli.

Leeks

Leeks taste better lightly steamed or sautéed rather than boiled, which can make them soggy. They are a key ingredient in hearty soups, and also combine well with eggs and cream in savory tarts. Baby leeks are delicious quickly roasted in a hot oven. They can also be sliced paper thin and added sparingly to salads.

Onions

Onions offer a range of taste sensations from the sweet and mild Bermuda onion and light, fresh-tasting scallion to the versatile and pungent yellow onion. Once cooked, the flavor becomes mellow—roasting is a particularly good way of bringing out their delicious sweetness. Small pearl onions are good cooked whole in a stew or braised; they are also useful for kebabs. Red and white onions are delicious thinly sliced and scattered over salads.

Shallots

Forming one of the smaller bulbs in the onion family, shallots have a distinctive sweet, piquant, and full-bodied flavor that forms the base of many classic French sauces. Shallots also feature in Southeast Asian cuisine, where they are deep-fried and used as a crisp topping for salads and rice dishes. Fresh shallots are at their peak in spring, but shallots dry well and the dried ones are available year round.

Mushroom & Barley Soup

Serves 4

ingredients

- ¼ cup pearl barley
- 6 cups vegetable stock
- 1 bay leaf
- 1 tbsp butter
- 5 cups thinly sliced mushrooms (about 12 oz/350 g)
- 1 tsp olive oil
- 1 onion, finely chopped
- 2 carrots, thinly sliced
- 1 tbsp chopped fresh tarragon, plus extra leaves to garnish
- 1 tbsp chopped fresh parsley, plus extra to garnish
- salt and pepper

1 Rinse the pearl barley and drain. Bring 2 cups of the stock to a boil in a small saucepan. Add the bay leaf and, if the stock is unsalted, add a large pinch of salt. Stir in the pearl barley, reduce the heat, cover, and simmer for 40 minutes.

2 Melt the butter in a large skillet over medium heat. Add the mushrooms and season to taste with salt and pepper. Cook, stirring occasionally at first and more often as the mushrooms start to color, for 8 minutes, until they are golden brown. Remove from the heat.

3 Heat the oil in a large saucepan over medium heat and add the onion and carrots. Cover and cook, stirring frequently, for 3 minutes, or until the onion is softened.

4 Add the remaining stock to the saucepan with the onion and carrots and bring to a boil. Stir in the pearl barley with its cooking liquid and add the mushrooms. Reduce the heat, cover, and simmer gently, stirring occasionally, for about 20 minutes, or until the carrots are tender.

5 Stir in the chopped tarragon and parsley. Taste and adjust the seasoning, adding salt and pepper, if needed. Ladle into warm bowls, garnish with chopped parsley and tarragon leaves, and serve.

Mixed Mushroom Pizza

Makes 2

ingredients
- 3 tbsp oil
- 2 garlic cloves, crushed
- 2 tbsp chopped fresh oregano
- 2 thin-and-crispy pizza crusts, 9-inches/23-cm in diameter
- ⅓ cup ricotta cheese
- 1 tbsp milk
- 3 tbsp butter
- 12 oz/350 g mixed mushrooms, sliced
- 2 tsp lemon juice
- 1 tbsp chopped fresh marjoram
- ¼ cup grated Parmesan cheese
- salt and pepper

1 Preheat the oven to 475°F/240°C. Mix 2 tablespoons of the oil, the garlic, and oregano together and brush over the pizza crusts.

2 Mix the ricotta cheese and milk together in a bowl. Season to taste with salt and pepper and spread the mixture over the pizza crusts, leaving an 1½-inch/4-cm border around the edges.

3 Heat the butter and the remaining oil together in a large skillet. Add the mushrooms and cook over high heat for 2 minutes. Remove the skillet from the heat, season to taste with salt and pepper, and stir in the lemon juice and marjoram.

4 Spoon the mushroom mixture over the pizza crusts, leaving a ½-inch/1-cm border. Sprinkle with the Parmesan cheese, then bake in the preheated oven for 12–15 minutes, until the crusts are crisp and the mushrooms are cooked. Serve immediately.

Linguine with Mushroom & Mascarpone Sauce

Serves 4

ingredients

- 1 lb/450 g dried linguine
- 4 tbsp butter
- 1 garlic clove, crushed
- 8 oz/225 g mixed wild mushrooms, sliced
- 9 oz/250 g mascarpone cheese
- 2 tbsp milk
- 1 tsp chopped fresh sage, plus extra leaves to garnish
- salt and pepper
- Parmesan cheese shavings, to serve

1 Bring a large saucepan of lightly salted water to a boil. Add the pasta, return to a boil, and cook for 8–10 minutes, or according to the package directions, until tender but still firm to the bite.

2 Meanwhile, melt the butter in a separate large saucepan. Add the garlic and mushrooms and cook for 3–4 minutes. Reduce the heat and stir in the mascarpone cheese, milk, and chopped sage. Season to taste with salt and pepper.

3 Drain the pasta thoroughly and add to the mushroom sauce. Toss until the pasta is well coated with the sauce. Transfer to warm dishes, garnish with sage leaves, and serve immediately with Parmesan cheese shavings.

Wild Mushroom Bruschetta

Serves 4

ingredients

- 4 slices sourdough bread
- 3 garlic cloves, 1 halved and
  2 crushed
- 2 tbsp extra virgin olive oil,
  plus extra for drizzling
- 8 oz/225 g mixed wild
  mushrooms, such as porcini,
  chanterelles, and portobello
  mushrooms
- 1 tbsp olive oil
- 2 tbsp butter
- 1 small onion or
  2 shallots, finely chopped
- 4 tbsp dry white wine
  or Marsala
- salt and pepper
- 2 tbsp coarsely chopped fresh
  flat-leaf parsley, to garnish

1 Preheat the broiler to medium. Toast the bread slices on both sides under the preheated broiler, rub with the garlic halves, and drizzle with the extra virgin olive oil. Transfer to a baking sheet and keep warm.

2 Wipe the mushrooms thoroughly to remove any trace of soil and slice any large ones. Heat the olive oil with half of the butter in a skillet, add the mushrooms, and cook over medium heat, stirring frequently, for 3–4 minutes, until soft. Remove with a slotted spoon and keep warm.

3 Heat the remaining butter in the skillet, add the onion and crushed garlic, and cook over medium heat, stirring frequently, for 3–4 minutes, until soft. Add the wine, stir well, and let simmer for 2–3 minutes, until reduced and thickened. Return the mushrooms to the skillet and heat through. The sauce should be thick enough to glaze the mushrooms. Season to taste with salt and pepper.

4 Pile the mushrooms on top of the toasted bread, scatter with the parsley, and serve immediately, drizzled with extra virgin olive oil.

Wild Mushroom Omelet

Serves 2

ingredients

- 1 tsp extra virgin olive oil
- 1 small onion, cut into wedges
- 2–3 garlic cloves, crushed
- 3 oz/85 g mixed wild mushrooms, halved if large
- 1¼ cups sliced button mushrooms
- 1 zucchini, grated
- 2 eggs
- 2 egg whites
- 2 tbsp water
- 1 yellow bell pepper, seeded and cut into strips
- 1 tbsp grated Parmesan cheese (optional)
- 1 tbsp shredded fresh basil
- pepper
- arugula, to garnish
- whole wheat bread, to serve

1 Heat the oil in a large nonstick skillet. Add the onion and garlic, cover, and cook, stirring occasionally, for 3 minutes. Add the mushrooms and cook for an additional 4–5 minutes, or until the mushrooms have softened slightly. Add the zucchini.

2 Beat together the whole eggs, egg whites, and water with pepper to taste. Pour into the skillet, increase the heat slightly, and cook, drawing the egg into the center of the skillet from the edges with a fork or spatula.

3 When the omelet is set on the bottom, sprinkle with the yellow bell pepper, followed by the Parmesan cheese, if using, and basil. Cook for another 3–4 minutes, or until set to personal preference.

4 Cut the omelet into wedges, garnish with arugula, and serve with whole wheat bread.

Mushroom Risotto

Serves 4

ingredients

- 2 oz/55 g dried wild mushrooms
- 1 cup warm water
- 3 cups vegetable stock
- 6 tbsp olive oil
- 10 oz/280 g mixed fresh wild or portobello mushrooms, thickly sliced
- 2 garlic cloves, finely chopped
- 1 tbsp finely chopped fresh thyme
- 1 onion, finely chopped
- heaping 1¾ cups risotto rice
- ⅔ cup dry white wine
- 4 tbsp butter
- scant 1¼ cups grated Parmesan cheese
- salt and pepper

1 Soak the dried mushrooms in the warm water in a small bowl for 10–15 minutes. Drain, reserving the soaking liquid (strain it thoroughly to remove any grit). Finely slice the drained mushrooms.

2 Bring the stock to a boil, then reduce the heat and keep simmering gently over low heat while you cook the risotto.

3 Heat half the oil in a deep skillet, add the fresh mushrooms, and cook over low heat, stirring occasionally, for 10–15 minutes, until soft. Add the dried mushrooms and garlic and cook, stirring frequently, for an additional 2–3 minutes. Add the thyme and salt and pepper to taste, then remove the mushroom mixture from the skillet and keep warm.

4 Meanwhile, heat the remaining oil in the saucepan, add the onion, and cook over low heat, stirring occasionally, for 10–12 minutes, until soft. Gently stir in the rice and cook, stirring, for 1 minute, until the rice is translucent and coated with the oil.

5 Pour in the wine and cook, stirring, until it has all been absorbed. Add the reserved soaking liquid and cook, stirring, until it has all been absorbed.

6 Gradually add the hot stock, a ladleful at a time, stirring continuously. Add more stock as the rice absorbs each addition. Increase the heat so the liquid simmers. Cook for 20–25 minutes, or until all the liquid has been absorbed and the rice is creamy but still firm to the bite.

7 Remove from the heat and gently stir in the mushroom mixture, butter, and half of the Parmesan cheese. Season to taste with salt and pepper.

8 Divide among warm plates and serve immediately, sprinkled with the remaining Parmesan cheese.

Creamy Stuffed Mushrooms

Serves 4

ingredients
- 1 oz/25 g dried porcini
- 1½ cups diced starchy potatoes, such as russets
- 2 tbsp melted butter
- 4 tbsp heavy cream
- 2 tbsp snipped fresh chives
- 8 portobello mushrooms
- ¼ cup grated Emmental cheese
- ⅔ cup vegetable stock
- salt and pepper

1 Preheat the oven to 425°F/220°C. Place the dried porcini in a small bowl. Add enough boiling water to cover and let soak for 20 minutes.

2 Meanwhile, cook the potatoes in a saucepan of lightly salted boiling water for 10 minutes, until cooked through and tender. Drain well and mash until smooth.

3 Drain the soaked porcini and then chop them finely. Mix them into the mashed potatoes.

4 Thoroughly blend the butter, cream, and chives together and pour into the potato mixture, mixing well. Season to taste with salt and pepper.

5 Remove the stems from the portobello mushrooms. Chop the stems and stir them into the potato mixture. Spoon the mixture into the mushrooms and sprinkle the cheese over the top.

6 Arrange the stuffed mushrooms in a shallow ovenproof dish and pour in the stock.

7 Cover the dish and cook in the preheated oven for 20 minutes. Uncover and cook for an additional 5 minutes, until golden. Serve the mushrooms immediately.

Creamed Morels on
Spinach & Cornmeal Cakes

Serves 6

ingredients
- 6 handfuls fresh morels
- 3 tbsp olive oil
- 4 shallots, finely chopped
- 2 garlic cloves, crushed
- scant ½ cup Marsala
- scant 1 cup heavy cream
- 2 tbsp whole-grain mustard
- 1 small bunch fresh tarragon, finely chopped, plus extra sprigs to garnish
- salt and pepper

cornmeal cakes
- 4 cups vegetable stock
- 1¾ cups cornmeal
- 1 cup grated Parmesan cheese
- 2 handfuls baby spinach, coarsely torn
- 2 tsp coarsely cracked black peppercorns
- scant ½ cup butter, softened
- salt and pepper
- olive oil, for oiling

1 To make the cornmeal cakes, bring the stock to a rapid boil and add the cornmeal in a steady stream, stirring quickly with a large balloon whisk. Cook according to the package directions.

2 Using a wooden spoon, stir in the Parmesan cheese, spinach, peppercorns, and half of the butter. Taste and adjust the seasoning, adding salt and pepper, if needed.

3 Lightly oil a baking sheet. Pour the cornmeal mixture out onto the prepared baking sheet, smooth over with a palette knife, and let cool. When the cornmeal has set, use a 4-inch/10-cm round pastry cutter to cut out 6 rounds.

4 Cut the morels in half and gently wash them, being careful to remove any traces of soil and grit. Dry gently with paper towels.

5 Heat the oil in a saucepan over medium heat, add the shallots and garlic, and cook for 3–4 minutes, until softened. Add the morels and cook, stirring continuously, for 2 minutes. Pour in the Marsala and simmer briefly, then add the cream, mustard, and chopped tarragon. Season to taste with salt and pepper. Keep warm.

6 Heat the remaining butter in a skillet over high heat, add the cornmeal cakes, and cook for 3–4 minutes on each side, until crisp and golden. Serve immediately, topped with the creamed morels and garnished with tarragon sprigs.

French Onion Soup

Serves 6

ingredients

- 3 tbsp olive oil
- 5¾ cups thinly sliced onions (about 1 lb 8 oz/675 g)
- 4 garlic cloves, 3 chopped and 1 halved
- 1 tsp sugar
- 2 tsp chopped fresh thyme, plus extra sprigs to garnish
- 2 tbsp all-purpose flour
- ½ cup white wine
- 8 cups vegetable stock
- 6 slices French bread
- 2¾ cups grated Gruyère cheese

1 Heat the oil in a large heavy-bottom saucepan, then add the onions and cook, stirring occasionally, for 10 minutes, until they are just beginning to brown. Stir in the chopped garlic, sugar, and chopped thyme, then reduce the heat and cook, stirring occasionally, for 30 minutes, or until the onions are golden brown.

2 Sprinkle in the flour and cook, stirring, for 1–2 minutes. Stir in the wine. Gradually stir in the stock and bring to a boil, skimming off any foam that rises to the surface, then reduce the heat and simmer for 45 minutes.

3 Meanwhile, preheat the broiler to medium. Toast the bread on both sides under the broiler. Rub the toast with the garlic halves.

4 Ladle the soup into 6 flameproof bowls set on a baking sheet. Float a piece of toast in each bowl and divide the cheese among them. Place under the preheated broiler for 2–3 minutes, or until the cheese has just melted. Garnish with thyme sprigs and serve immediately.

Flatbread with Onion & Rosemary

Makes 1 loaf

ingredients

- 3⅓ cups white bread flour, plus extra for dusting
- 1½ tsp active dry yeast
- ½ tsp salt
- 2 tbsp chopped fresh rosemary, plus extra small sprigs to garnish
- 5 tbsp extra virgin olive oil, plus extra for oiling
- 1¼ cups warm water
- 1 red onion, finely sliced and separated into rings
- 1 tbsp sea salt

1 Mix the flour, yeast, and salt together in a mixing bowl, then stir in the chopped rosemary. Make a well in the center. Mix 3 tablespoons of the oil and the water together in a pitcher and pour into the well. Gradually mix the liquid into the flour mixture with a palette knife. Gather the mixture together with your hands to form a soft dough.

2 Turn out the dough onto a lightly floured work surface and knead for 8–10 minutes, until smooth and elastic. Return the dough to the bowl, cover with a clean dish towel or oiled plastic wrap, and let rise in a warm place for 45 minutes–1 hour, or until doubled in size.

3 Preheat the oven to 400°F/200°C. Oil a baking sheet. Turn out the dough and knead for 1 minute, until smooth. Gently roll out the dough to a round about 12 inches/30 cm in diameter; it doesn't have to be a perfect circle—a slightly oval shape is traditional.

4 Transfer to the prepared baking sheet, cover with a clean dish towel or oiled plastic wrap, and let rise in a warm place for 20–30 minutes.

5 Make holes about 2 inches/5 cm apart all over the surface of the dough with the handle of a wooden spoon. Spread the onion rings over the dough, drizzle with the remaining oil, and sprinkle with the salt.

6 Bake in the preheated oven for 20 minutes, then scatter the rosemary sprigs over the top and bake for another 5 minutes, until well risen and golden brown. Transfer to a wire rack to cool slightly, then serve warm.

Caramelized Onion Tart

Serves 6–8

ingredients

- scant ½ cup unsalted butter
- 5¼ cups thinly sliced onions (about 1 lb 5 oz/600 g)
- 2 eggs
- scant ½ cup heavy cream
- 1 cup grated Gruyère cheese
- 8-inch/20-cm prepared pastry shell
- 1 cup coarsely grated Parmesan cheese
- salt and pepper

1 Melt the butter in a heavy-bottom skillet over medium heat. Add the onions and cook, stirring frequently to avoid burning, for 30 minutes, or until browned and caramelized. Remove the onions from the skillet and set aside.

2 Preheat the oven to 375°F/190°C. Beat the eggs in a large bowl, stir in the cream, and season to taste with salt and pepper. Add the Gruyère cheese and mix well. Stir in the cooked onions.

3 Pour the egg and onion mixture into the pastry shell and sprinkle with the Parmesan cheese. Place on a baking sheet and bake in the preheated oven for 15–20 minutes, until the filling has set and is beginning to brown.

4 Remove from the oven and let rest for at least 10 minutes. The tart can be served hot or left to cool to room temperature.

Onion Dhal

Serves 4

ingredients
- ½ cup red split lentils
- 6 tbsp vegetable oil
- 1 small bunch scallions, chopped
- 1 tsp finely chopped fresh ginger
- 1 tsp crushed garlic
- 1½ tsp chili powder
- 1½ tsp turmeric
- 1¼ cups water
- 1 tsp salt
- 1 fresh green chile, seeded and finely chopped
- chopped fresh cilantro, to garnish

1 Rinse the lentils thoroughly and set aside until required.

2 Heat the oil in a heavy-bottom saucepan. Add the scallions to the pan and fry over medium heat, stirring frequently, until lightly browned.

3 Reduce the heat and add the ginger, garlic, chili powder, and turmeric. Briefly stir-fry the scallions with the spices. Add the lentils and stir to blend.

4 Add the water to the lentil mixture, reduce the heat to low, and cook for 20–25 minutes.

5 When the lentils are tender, add the salt and stir gently to mix well.

6 Transfer the onion dhal to a serving dish. Stir in the chile and serve immediately, garnished with fresh cilantro.

Scallion, Pea
& Ricotta Tartlets

Makes 12

ingredients

tartlet dough
- 1⅔ cups all-purpose flour, plus extra for dusting
- pinch of salt
- heaping ½ cup butter, diced, plus extra for greasing
- 1 egg yolk

filling
- 9 oz/250 g ricotta cheese
- 3½ oz/100 g Pecorino Romano cheese
- 1 egg, beaten
- 12 scallions, finely chopped
- 2 tbsp fresh shelled peas, lightly cooked and cooled
- 1 tsp green peppercorns in brine, drained
- salt and pepper

1 To make the dough, sift the flour and salt together into a bowl, add the butter, and rub in with your fingertips until the mixture resembles fine breadcrumbs. Add the egg yolk and enough cold water to form a smooth dough. Cover and chill in the refrigerator for 30 minutes.

2 Preheat the oven to 375°F/190°C. Lightly grease a deep 12-cup muffin pan.

3 Roll the pastry out on a floured work surface to a thickness of about ⅛ inch/3 mm. Using a pastry cutter, stamp out rounds large enough to line the cups of the muffin pan. Gently press the pastry shells into the cups. Line each pastry shell with a small piece of parchment paper and fill with pie weights or dried beans.

4 Bake the pastry shells in the preheated oven for 4–5 minutes, until golden and crisp. Remove the paper and weights.

5 Meanwhile, to make the filling, mix the ricotta and Pecorino Romano cheeses together in a large bowl. Add the egg, scallions, and peas. Chop the peppercorns finely, then add to the mixture. Season to taste with salt and pepper.

6 Spoon the filling into the pastry shells and bake for 10 minutes, or until golden. Serve warm.

Leek & Potato Soup

Serves 4

ingredients
- 2 tbsp butter
- 2 garlic cloves, chopped
- 3 large leeks, sliced
- 4 potatoes, cut into
  bite-size chunks
- 2 tbsp chopped fresh parsley
- 1 tbsp chopped fresh oregano
- 1 bay leaf
- 3½ cups vegetable stock
- scant 1 cup light cream
- 1 cup greated firm smoked
  cheese
- salt and pepper
- snipped fresh chives, to garnish

1 Melt the butter in a large saucepan over medium heat. Add the garlic and cook, stirring, for 1 minute. Add the leeks and cook, stirring, for 2 minutes. Add the potatoes, half of the parsley, the oregano, bay leaf, and stock, then season to taste with salt and pepper.

2 Bring to a boil, then reduce the heat, cover the saucepan, and let simmer for 25 minutes. Remove from the heat, let cool for 10 minutes, then remove and discard the bay leaf.

3 Transfer half of the soup to a food processor and process until smooth (you may need to do this in batches). Return to the saucepan with the rest of the soup, stir in the cream, and reheat gently. Adjust the seasoning, adding salt and pepper, if needed.

4 Remove from the heat and stir in the cheese. Ladle into serving bowls. Garnish with the remaining parsley and the chives, and serve immediately.

Leeks with Yellow Bean Sauce

Serves 4

ingredients

- 1 lb/450 g leeks
- 12 baby corn
- 6 scallions
- 3 tbsp peanut oil
- 2⅓ cups shredded Chinese cabbage
- 4 tbsp yellow bean sauce

1 Using a sharp knife, slice the leeks, halve the baby corn, and cut the scallions into 1-inch/2.5-cm lengths.

2 Heat a wok or skillet, then add the oil and heat until it is smoking.

3 Add the leeks, Chinese cabbage, and baby corn to the wok. Stir-fry the vegetables over high heat for about 5 minutes, or until the edges of the vegetables are slightly brown.

4 Add the scallions to the wok, stirring to combine.

5 Stir in the yellow bean sauce. Continue to stir-fry the mixture in the wok for an additional 2 minutes, until the yellow bean sauce is heated through and the vegetables are thoroughly coated in the sauce.

6 Transfer the stir-fried vegetables and sauce to warm serving dishes and serve immediately.

Chilled Garlic Soup

Serves 4–6

ingredients

- 16 slices day-old country-style white bread, crusts removed, torn
- 5 large garlic cloves, halved
- ½ cup extra virgin olive oil, plus extra for drizzling
- 4–5 tbsp sherry vinegar
- heaping 3 cups ground almonds
- 5 cups chilled water
- salt and white pepper
- seedless white grapes, halved to garnish

1 Put the bread in a bowl with just enough cold water to cover and let soak for 15 minutes. Squeeze the bread dry and transfer to a food processor.

2 Add the garlic, oil, vinegar to taste, and the ground almonds to the food processor with 1 cup of the water and process until blended.

3 With the motor running, slowly pour in the remaining water until a smooth soup forms. Taste and add extra vinegar, if needed. Cover and chill for at least 4 hours.

4 To serve, stir well and adjust the seasoning, adding salt and white pepper, if needed. Ladle into bowls, drizzle with a little oil, and float grapes on top. Serve immediately.

Garlic Spaghetti

Serves 4

ingredients
- scant ½ cup olive oil
- 3 garlic cloves, crushed
- 1 lb/450 g dried spaghetti
- 3 tbsp coarsely chopped fresh parsley
- salt and pepper

1 Heat the oil in a medium saucepan. Add the garlic and cook over low heat, stirring continuously, until golden brown, then remove the pan from the heat. Do not let the garlic burn because this will taint its flavor.

2 Meanwhile, bring a large saucepan of lightly salted water to the boil. Add the spaghetti, return to a boil, and cook for 8–10 minutes, or according to the package directions, until the spaghetti is tender but still firm to the bite. Drain thoroughly and return to the pan.

3 Add the oil-and-garlic mixture to the spaghetti and toss to coat thoroughly. Season to taste with pepper, add the parsley, and toss well to coat again.

4 Transfer the spaghetti to a warm serving dish and serve immediately.

Chapter 5
Peas, Beans, Lentils & Corn

Directory of Peas, Beans, Lentils & Corn

These members of the legume family, along with corn, are invaluable staples in the cook's kitchen, not least because many of them may be dried to increase their shelf life. They are also a useful source of vegetable protein.

Bean sprouts

Packed with nutrients, these are the crisp, juicy shoots most commonly sprouted from mung beans. They are delicious raw in salads, or cooked briefly in a stir-fry until barely wilted.

Cannellini bean

These small, ivory beans have a creamy texture when cooked. They are delicious in salads, soups, and stews, and can be pureed to make a nutritious alternative to mashed potatoes.

Chickpea

Also known as gabanzo beans, chickpeas resemble shelled hazelnuts and have a nutty flavor and a creamy texture. They are widely used in Indian and Middle Eastern cuisines.

Corn

A freshly picked ear of corn is perfect plainly boiled and tossed with a little melted butter. Unlike other vegetables, corn toughens if overcooked. Young ears need about 3 minutes in rapidly boiling unsalted water.

Fava bean

Fresh fava beans have a unique flavor and are best lightly cooked if they are not to become mealy. Remove the outer skin after cooking if it is tough. They are delicious steamed and tossed with butter and lemon zest.

Flageolet bean and cranberry bean

The pretty, pale green flageolet bean has a delicate flavor and soft texture, while the hearty cranberry bean is pinkish-brown with a sweetish flavor and firmer texture. It is often used in Italian bean and pasta soups.

Green bean and runner bean

Both green beans and runner beans are delicately flavored and benefit from steaming rather than boiling. Runner beans usually have to have their strings removed, but most green beans nowadays are stringless and simply need to be trimmed. They are delicious simply anointed with butter, or served in salads.

Kidney bean

Kidney beans have a soft, mealy texture. They are essential for chili con carne and Mexican refried beans.

Lentil

Brown lentils have a robust texture and flavor, and add substance to stews, stuffings, and soups. Green lentils and French Puy lentils are similar to the brown lentil, but have a slightly milder flavor. The tiny, dark gray-green Puy lentil, available from online suppliers, is considered superior in flavor to other varieties. They are delicious in warm salads with a vinaigrette dressing and also make a hearty addition to stews. If you can't find these, use green lentils as a substitute. Red split lentils are ideal for thickening soups and stews, and are used to make the Indian dish dahl.

Lima bean

These large, flat, cream-colored beans have a mealy texture when cooked. They are excellent with a garlicky tomato sauce as an accompaniment to roasted lamb.

Pea

Fresh garden peas are incredibly versatile and can be cooked quickly, either by steaming or boiling. They may be shelled so you eat only the seeds, or in the case of snow peas and snap peas, the pods are eaten along with the seeds. Dried split peas are interchangeable with red split lentils, although they need presoaking and take longer to cook. They are perfect for dahls, soups, casseroles, and purees.

Soybean

Soybeans range in color from creamy yellow to brownish-black. They are rich in protein and make a healthy addition to vegetarian dishes. They are used in a wide variety of foods including tofu, meat-replacement protein products, soy sauce, and miso paste. They are also an essential ingredient in Asian sauces, including black or yellow bean sauce, and hoisin sauce.

Chilled Pea Soup

Serves 3–4

ingredients
- 2 cups vegetable stock or water
- 3 cups frozen peas
- 1 cup finely chopped scallions
- 1¼ cups plain yogurt or light cream
- salt and pepper

to serve
- 1 tbsp extra virgin olive oil
- 2 tbsp chopped fresh mint
- 2 tbsp snipped fresh chives
- grated rind of ½ lemon

1 Bring the stock to a boil in a large saucepan over medium heat. Reduce the heat, add the peas and scallions, and simmer for 5 minutes.

2 Let cool slightly, then strain twice, making sure that you remove any small pieces of skin. Pour into a large bowl, season to taste with salt and pepper, and stir in the yogurt. Cover the bowl with plastic wrap, and chill in the refrigerator for several hours.

3 To serve, remove from the refrigerator, mix well, and ladle into individual serving bowls. Drizzle with the oil and sprinkle with the mint, chives, and lemon rind. Serve immediately.

Lemon Beans

Serves 4

ingredients
- 2 lb/900 g mixed fresh beans, such as shelled fava beans, green beans, and runner beans
- 5 tbsp butter or margarine
- ¼ cup all-purpose flour
- 1¼ cups vegetable stock
- 5 tbsp dry white wine
- 6 tbsp light cream
- 3 tbsp chopped fresh mixed herbs
- grated rind of 1 lemon
- 2 tbsp lemon juice
- salt and pepper
- strips of lemon zest, to garnish

1 Cook the beans in a saucepan of boiling salted water for 10 minutes, or until tender. Drain and place in a warm serving dish.

2 Meanwhile, melt the butter in a saucepan. Add the flour and cook, stirring continuously, for 1 minute. Remove the pan from the heat and gradually stir in the stock and wine. Return the pan to the heat and bring to a boil, stirring.

3 Remove the pan from the heat once again and stir in the cream, herbs, and lemon rind and juice. Season to taste with salt and pepper. Pour the sauce over the beans, mixing well to coat thoroughly. Serve immediately, garnished with strips of lemon zest.

Spaghetti with Fresh Pea
Pesto & Fava Beans

Serves 4

ingredients
- 1⅔ cups fresh shelled fava beans
- 1 lb 2 oz/500 g dried spaghetti
- salt and pepper

pea pesto
- 3 cups fresh shelled peas
- 5 tbsp extra virgin olive oil
- 2 garlic cloves, crushed
- 1 cup grated Parmesan cheese, plus extra shavings to serve
- ¾ cup chopped, blanched almonds
- pinch of sugar
- salt and pepper

1 For the pesto, cook the peas in a saucepan of boiling water for 2–3 minutes, until just tender. Drain and transfer to a blender or food processor. Add the oil, garlic, and Parmesan cheese and process to a coarse paste. Add the almonds and process again. Add the sugar and season to taste with salt and pepper. Set aside.

2 Blanch the fava beans in a saucepan of boiling salted water for 2–3 minutes, until just tender. Drain and let cool. Peel off the gray skins.

3 Bring a large saucepan of lightly salted water to a boil. Add the spaghetti, return to a boil, and cook for 8–10 minutes, or according to the package directions, until the spaghetti is tender but still firm to the bite.

4 Drain the spaghetti and return to the pan with the fava beans and pea pesto. Toss well and transfer to individual serving plates. Grind over a little pepper, top with the Parmesan shavings, and serve immediately.

Potato & Split Pea Soup

Serves 4

ingredients
- 2 tbsp vegetable oil
- 4 starchy potatoes, such as russets, in their skins, diced
- 2 onions, diced
- ⅓ cup split green peas
- 4 cups vegetable stock
- ½ cup grated Gruyère cheese
- salt and pepper

croutons
- 3 tbsp butter
- 1 garlic clove, crushed
- 1 tbsp chopped fresh parsley
- 1 thick slice white bread, diced

1 Heat the oil in a large saucepan. Add the potatoes and onions and cook over medium heat, stirring continuously, for about 5 minutes.

2 Add the split green peas to the pan and stir together well.

3 Pour the stock into the pan and bring to a boil. Reduce the heat to low and simmer for about 35 minutes, until the potatoes are tender and the split peas are cooked.

4 Meanwhile, make the croutons. Melt the butter in a skillet. Add the garlic, parsley, and bread and cook, turning frequently, for about 2 minutes, until golden all over.

5 Stir the cheese into the soup and season to taste with salt and pepper. Heat gently until the cheese is starting to melt.

6 Pour the soup into warm soup bowls and sprinkle the croutons on top. Serve immediately.

Fava Beans with Feta

Serves 4–6

ingredients
- 3⅓ cups shelled fava beans
- 4 tbsp extra virgin olive oil
- 1 tbsp lemon juice
- 1 tbsp finely chopped fresh dill, plus extra to garnish
- 2 oz/55 g feta cheese, diced
- salt and pepper

1 Bring a large saucepan of lightly salted water to a boil. Add the fava beans and cook for 2–3 minutes, until tender. Drain thoroughly and set aside.

2 When the beans are cool enough to handle, remove and discard the gray skins. Put the peeled beans in a serving bowl.

3 Combine the oil and lemon juice in a small bowl, then season to taste with salt and pepper. Pour the dressing over the warm beans, add the dill, and stir gently. Adjust the seasoning, adding salt and pepper, if needed.

4 If serving hot, add the cheese, toss gently, and sprinkle with dill, then serve immediately. Alternatively, set aside the beans in their dressing to cool and then chill until required. To serve cold, remove from the refrigerator 10 minutes before serving to bring to room temperature. Taste and adjust the seasoning, adding salt and pepper, if needed, then sprinkle with the cheese and dill.

Green Bean Salad with Feta

Serves 4

ingredients

- 12 oz/350 g green beans, trimmed
- 1 red onion, chopped
- 3–4 tbsp chopped fresh cilantro
- 2 radishes, thinly sliced
- ½ cup crumbled feta cheese
- 1 tsp chopped fresh oregano or ½ tsp dried oregano
- 2 tbsp red wine or fruit vinegar
- 5 tbsp extra virgin olive oil
- 3 ripe tomatoes, cut into wedges
- pepper

1 Pour about 2 inches/5 cm of water into the bottom of a steamer or medium saucepan and bring to a boil. Add the beans to the top of the steamer or place them in a metal colander set over the pan of water. Cover and steam for about 5 minutes, until just tender.

2 Transfer the beans to a bowl and add the onion, cilantro, radishes, and cheese.

3 Sprinkle the oregano over the salad, then season to taste with pepper. Whisk the vinegar and oil together and pour over the salad. Toss gently to mix well.

4 Transfer to a serving platter, add the tomato wedges, and serve immediately or chill in the refrigerator until ready to serve.

Cheesy Corn Fritters

Makes 8–10

ingredients
- 1 egg
- scant 1 cup milk
- heaping ¾ cup all-purpose flour
- ½ tsp baking powder
- ⅓ cup drained canned corn kernels
- ¼ cup grated cheddar cheese
- 1 tsp snipped fresh chives
- 2 tsp sunflower oil

1 Put the egg and milk into a small bowl and beat with a fork.

2 Add the flour and baking powder and beat until smooth. Stir in the corn kernels, cheese, and chives.

3 Heat the oil in a nonstick skillet over medium heat. Drop in either teaspoonfuls or tablespoonfuls of the batter.

4 Cook for 1–2 minutes on each side, until the fritters are puffed up and golden. Drain on paper towels and serve.

Corn, Potato & Cheese Soup

Serves 6

ingredients

- 2 tbsp butter
- 2 shallots, finely chopped
- 2 potatoes, diced
- ¼ cup all-purpose flour
- 2 tbsp dry white wine
- 1¼ cups milk
- 11½ oz/325 g canned corn kernels, drained
- ¾ cup grated Gruyère, Emmental, or cheddar cheese
- 8–10 fresh sage leaves, chopped, plus extra sprigs to garnish
- scant 2 cups heavy cream

croutons

- 2–3 slices day-old white bread
- 2 tbsp olive oil

1 To make the croutons, cut the crusts off the bread slices, then cut the remaining bread into ¼-inch/5-mm cubes. Heat the oil in a heavy-bottom skillet and add the bread cubes. Cook, tossing and stirring continuously, until evenly colored. Drain the croutons thoroughly on paper towels and reserve.

2 Melt the butter in a large heavy-bottom saucepan. Add the shallots and cook over low heat, stirring occasionally, for 5 minutes, or until softened. Add the potatoes and cook, stirring, for 2 minutes.

3 Sprinkle in the flour and cook, stirring, for 1 minute. Remove the saucepan from the heat and stir in the wine, then gradually stir in the milk. Return the saucepan to the heat and bring to a boil, stirring continuously, then reduce the heat and simmer.

4 Stir in the corn, cheese, chopped sage, and cream and heat through gently until the cheese has just melted.

5 Ladle the soup into warm bowls, scatter with the croutons, garnish with sage sprigs, and serve immediately.

Bean Sprout Salad

Serves 4

ingredients

- 4 cups fresh bean sprouts (about 12 oz/350 g)
- 1 small cucumber
- 1 green bell pepper, seeded and cut into matchsticks
- 1 carrot, cut into matchsticks
- 2 tomatoes, finely chopped
- 1 celery stalk, cut into matchsticks
- 1 garlic clove, crushed
- dash of chili sauce
- 2 tbsp light soy sauce
- 1 tsp wine vinegar
- 2 tsp sesame oil
- fresh chives, to garnish

1 Blanch the bean sprouts in boiling water for 1 minute. Drain well and rinse under cold water. Drain thoroughly again.

2 Cut the cucumber in half lengthwise. Scoop out the seeds with a teaspoon and discard. Cut the flesh into matchsticks and mix with the bean sprouts, green bell pepper, carrot, tomatoes, and celery.

3 Mix together the garlic, chili sauce, soy sauce, vinegar, and sesame oil. Pour the dressing over the vegetables, tossing well to coat. Spoon onto individual serving plates. Garnish with chives and serve.

Tuscan Beans on Ciabatta Toast with Fresh Herbs

Serves 2

ingredients
- 4 slices ciabatta bread
- 1 tbsp olive oil
- 1 small onion, finely diced
- 1 garlic clove, crushed
- 9 oz/250 g canned lima beans, drained and rinsed
- 6 tbsp water
- 1 tbsp tomato paste
- 1 tsp balsamic vinegar
- 1 tbsp chopped fresh parsley
- 1 tbsp torn fresh basil
- salt and pepper

1 Preheat the broiler to medium. Place the ciabatta on a piece of aluminum foil on the rack in the broiler pan. Broil until lightly browned, then turn and cook on the other side.

2 Meanwhile, heat the oil in a medium saucepan, add the onion, and cook over low heat until soft. Add the garlic and cook for an additional 1 minute, then add the lima beans, water, and tomato paste. Bring to a boil, stirring occasionally, and cook for 2 minutes.

3 Add the vinegar, parsley, and basil and stir to combine. Season to taste with salt and pepper and serve over the slices of toasted ciabatta.

Hummus Toasts with Olives

Serves 4

ingredients
- 14 oz/400 g canned chickpeas
- juice of 1 large lemon
- 6 tbsp tahini
- 6 tsp olive oil
- 2 garlic cloves, crushed
- salt and pepper
- chopped fresh cilantro and chopped pitted black olives, to garnish

toasts
- 1 ciabatta loaf, sliced
- 2 garlic cloves, crushed
- 1 tbsp chopped fresh cilantro
- 4 tbsp olive oil

1 To make the hummus, first drain the chickpeas, reserving a little of the liquid. Put the chickpeas in a food processor and blend, gradually adding the reserved liquid and lemon juice. Blend well after each addition until smooth.

2 Stir in the tahini and 5 teaspoons of the oil. Add the garlic, season to taste with salt and pepper, and blend again until smooth.

3 Spoon the hummus into a serving dish. Drizzle the remaining oil over the top and garnish with cilantro and olives. Leave to chill in the refrigerator while preparing the toasts.

4 Preheat the broiler. Place the slices of ciabatta on a broiler rack in a single layer. Mix the garlic, cilantro, and oil together and drizzle over the bread slices. Cook under the preheated broiler for 2–3 minutes, turning once, until golden brown. Serve hot with the hummus.

Falafel Burgers

Serves 4

ingredients
- 1 lb 12 oz/800 g canned chickpeas, drained and rinsed
- 1 small onion, chopped
- juice and rind of 1 lime
- 2 tsp ground coriander
- 2 tsp ground cumin
- heaping 1/3 cup all-purpose flour
- 4 tbsp olive oil
- watercress, to garnish
- tomato salsa, to serve

1 Put the chickpeas, onion, lime juice and rind, and the spices into a food processor and process to a coarse paste.

2 Turn the mixture out onto a clean work surface or cutting board and shape into 4 patties.

3 Spread the flour out on a large flat plate and use to coat the patties.

4 Heat the oil in a large skillet, add the patties, and cook for 2 minutes on each side, until crisp. Garnish with watercress and serve with tomato salsa.

Mixed Bean &
Vegetable Crisp

Serves 4

ingredients
- 1 large onion, chopped
- ½ cup rinsed and drained canned red kidney beans
- ½ cup rinsed and drained canned lima beans
- ½ cup rinsed and drained canned chickpeas
- 2 zucchini, coarsely chopped
- 2 large carrots, coarsely chopped
- 4 tomatoes, peeled and coarsely chopped
- 2 celery stalks, chopped
- 1¼ cups vegetable stock
- 2 tbsp tomato paste
- salt and pepper

crispy topping
- 2 cups whole wheat breadcrumbs
- ¼ cup finely chopped hazelnuts
- heaping 1 tbsp chopped fresh parsley
- 1 cup grated cheddar cheese

1 Preheat the oven to 350°F/180°C.

2 Put the onion, kidney beans, lima beans, chickpeas, zucchini, carrots, tomatoes, and celery in a large ovenproof dish. Mix together the stock and tomato paste and pour over the vegetables. Season to taste with salt and pepper. Transfer to the preheated oven and bake for 15 minutes.

3 Meanwhile, to make the crispy topping, put the breadcrumbs in a large bowl, add the hazelnuts, parsley, and cheese, and mix together well.

4 Remove the vegetables from the oven and carefully sprinkle the crispy topping over the top. Do not press it down or it will sink into the vegetables and become mushy.

5 Return the vegetables to the oven and bake for 30 minutes, or until the crispy topping is golden brown. Remove from the oven and serve hot.

Vegetable Chili

Serves 4

ingredients

- 1 eggplant, peeled, if desired, cut into 1-inch/2.5-cm slices
- 1 tbsp olive oil, plus extra for brushing
- 1 large red or yellow onion, finely chopped
- 2 red or yellow bell peppers, seeded and finely chopped
- 3–4 garlic cloves, finely chopped or crushed
- 1 lb 12 oz/800 g canned chopped tomatoes
- 1 tbsp mild chili powder, or to taste
- ½ tsp ground cumin
- ½ tsp dried oregano
- 2 small zucchini, quartered lengthwise and sliced
- 14 oz/400 g canned kidney beans, drained and rinsed
- 2 cups water
- 1 tbsp tomato paste
- salt and pepper
- chopped scallions and grated cheddar cheese, to serve

1 Brush the eggplant slices on one side with oil. Heat half of the oil in a large heavy-bottom skillet over medium–high heat. Add the eggplant slices, oiled-side up, and cook for 5–6 minutes, until browned on one side. Turn the slices over, cook on the other side until browned, and transfer to a plate. Cut into bite-size pieces.

2 Heat the remaining oil in a large saucepan over medium heat. Add the onion and bell peppers and cook, stirring occasionally, for 3–4 minutes, until the onion is just softened but not browned. Add the garlic and continue cooking for 2–3 minutes, or until the onion is just beginning to color.

3 Add the tomatoes, chili powder, cumin, and oregano. Season to taste with salt and pepper. Bring just to a boil, reduce the heat, cover, and simmer gently for 15 minutes.

4 Add the zucchini, eggplant, and beans. Stir in the water and the tomato paste. Bring back to a boil, then cover the pan and continue simmering for about 45 minutes, or until the vegetables are tender. Taste and then adjust the seasoning, adding salt and pepper, if needed. If you prefer a hotter dish, stir in a little more chili powder.

5 Ladle into warm bowls and top with the scallions and cheese.

Kidney Bean Risotto

Serves 4

ingredients

- 4 tbsp olive oil
- 1 onion, chopped
- 2 garlic cloves, finely chopped
- 1 cup brown rice
- 2½ cup vegetable stock
- 1 red bell pepper, seeded and chopped
- 2 celery stalks, sliced
- 3⅔ cups thinly sliced cremini mushrooms
- 15 oz/425 g canned red kidney beans, drained and rinsed
- 3 tbsp chopped fresh parsley, plus extra to garnish
- scant ½ cup cashew nuts
- salt and pepper

1 Heat half of the oil in a large heavy-bottom saucepan. Add the onion and cook, stirring occasionally, for 5 minutes, or until soft. Add half of the garlic and cook, stirring frequently, for 2 minutes, then add the rice and stir for 1 minute, or until the grains are thoroughly coated with the oil.

2 Add the stock and bring to a boil, stirring continuously. Reduce the heat, cover, and simmer for 35–40 minutes, or until all the liquid has been absorbed.

3 Meanwhile, heat the remaining oil in a heavy-bottom skillet. Add the red bell pepper and celery and cook, stirring frequently, for 5 minutes. Add the mushrooms and the remaining garlic and cook, stirring frequently, for 4–5 minutes.

4 Stir the rice into the skillet. Add the beans, parsley, and nuts. Season to taste with salt and pepper and cook, stirring continously, until piping hot. Transfer to a warm serving dish, sprinkle with parsley, and serve.

Warm Red Lentil Salad
with Goat Cheese

Serves 4

ingredients
- 2 tbsp olive oil
- 2 tsp cumin seeds
- 2 garlic cloves, crushed
- 2 tsp grated fresh ginger
- heaping 1½ cups red split lentils
- 3 cups vegetable stock
- 2 tbsp chopped fresh mint
- 2 tbsp chopped fresh cilantro
- 2 red onions, thinly sliced
- 7 oz/200 g baby spinach leaves
- 1 tsp hazelnut oil
- 5½ oz/150 g soft goat cheese
- ¼ cup Greek yogurt
- pepper
- lemon wedges, to garnish
- toasted rye bread, to serve

1 Heat half of the olive oil in a large saucepan over medium heat, add the cumin seeds, garlic, and ginger, and cook, stirring continuously, for 2 minutes.

2 Stir in the lentils, then add the stock, a ladleful at a time, until it is all absorbed, stirring continuouslly—this will take about 20 minutes. Remove from the heat and stir in the herbs.

3 Meanwhile, heat the remaining olive oil in a skillet over medium heat, add the onions, and cook, stirring frequently, for 10 minutes, or until soft and lightly browned.

4 Place the spinach in a bowl, pour over the hazelnut oil, and toss well, then divide among individual serving plates.

5 Mash the goat cheese with the yogurt in a small bowl and season to taste with pepper.

6 Divide the lentils among the plates and top with the onions and the goat cheese mixture. Garnish with lemon wedges and serve with toasted rye bread.

Sweet Potato Curry
with Lentils

Serves 4

ingredients

- 1 tsp vegetable oil
- ¾ cup bite-size sweet potato cubes
- ½ cup bite-size potato cubes
- 1 small onion, finely chopped
- 1 small garlic clove, finely chopped
- 1 small fresh green chile, seeded and chopped
- ½ tsp ground ginger
- ¼ cup green lentils
- 5–7 tbsp hot vegetable stock
- ½ tsp garam masala
- 1 tbsp plain yogurt
- pepper

1 Heat the oil in a saucepan with a lid and sauté the sweet potato over medium heat, turning occasionally, for 5 minutes.

2 Meanwhile, cook the potato in a saucepan of boiling water for 6 minutes, until almost cooked. Drain and set aside.

3 Remove the sweet potato from the pan with a slotted spoon, then add the onion to the pan. Cook, stirring occasionally, for 5 minutes, or until transparent. Add the garlic, chile, and ginger and stir for 1 minute.

4 Return the sweet potato to the pan with the boiled potato, and add the lentils, 5 tablespoons of the stock, the garam masala, and pepper to taste. Stir well to combine, bring to a simmer, and cover.

5 Reduce the heat and simmer for 20 minutes, adding a little more stock if the curry looks too dry. Stir in the yogurt and serve.

Conversion Charts

temperatures

FAHRENHEIT (°F)	CELSIUS (°C)
225	110
250	120
275	140
300	150
325	160
350	180
375	190
400	200
425	220
450	230
475	240

weight measures

US STANDARD	METRIC
⅛ OZ	5 G
¼ OZ	10 G
½ OZ	15 G
1 OZ	25/30 G
1¼ OZ	35 G
1½ OZ	40 G
1¾ OZ	50 G
2 OZ	55 G
2¼ OZ	60 G
2½ OZ	70 G
3 OZ	85 G
3¼ OZ	90 G
3½ OZ	100 G
4 OZ	115 G
4½ OZ	125 G
5 OZ	140 G
5½ OZ	150 G
6 OZ	175 G
7 OZ	200 G
8 OZ	225 G
9 OZ	250 G
9¾ OZ	275 G
10 OZ	280 G
10½ OZ	300 G
11½ OZ	325 G
12 OZ	350 G
13 OZ	375 G
14 OZ	400 G
15 OZ	425 G
1 LB	450 G
1 LB 2 OZ	500 G

volume measures

US STANDARD	METRIC
¼ TSP	1.25 ML
½ TSP	2.5 ML
1 TSP	5 ML
2 TSP	10 ML
1 TBSP/3 TSP	15 ML
2 TBSP/1 FL OZ	30 ML
3 TBSP	45 ML
¼ CUP/4 TBSP/2 FL OZ	60 ML
⅓ CUP/5⅓ TBSP/2¾ FL OZ	80 ML
½ CUP/8 TBSP/4 FL OZ	120 ML
⅔ CUP/10⅔ TBSP/5 FL OZ	150 ML
¾ CUP/12 TBSP/6 FL OZ	175 ML
1 CUP/16 TBSP/8 FL OZ	240 ML
1¼ CUPS/10 FL OZ	300 ML
1½ CUPS/12 FL OZ	350 ML
2 CUPS/1 PT/16 FL OZ	450 ML
3 CUPS/24 FL OZ	700 ML
4 CUPS/1 QUART	950 ML
1.06 QUARTS	1 LITER
4 QUARTS/1 GALLON	3.8 LITERS